CW01371203

SENDING MY LAUNDRY FORWARD

SENDING MY LAUNDRY FORWARD

A Staff Officer's Account of the First Gulf War

Stuart Crawford

Copyright © 2014 Stuart Crawford

The moral right of the author has been asserted.

Apart from any fair dealing for the purposes of research or private study, or criticism or review, as permitted under the Copyright, Designs and Patents Act 1988, this publication may only be reproduced, stored or transmitted, in any form or by any means, with the prior permission in writing of the publishers, or in the case of reprographic reproduction in accordance with the terms of licences issued by the Copyright Licensing Agency. Enquiries concerning reproduction outside those terms should be sent to the publishers.

Matador
9 Priory Business Park
Kibworth Beauchamp
Leicestershire LE8 0RX, UK
Tel: (+44) 116 279 2299
Fax: (+44) 116 279 2277
Email: books@troubador.co.uk
Web: www.troubador.co.uk/matador

ISBN 978 1783064 182

British Library Cataloguing in Publication Data.
A catalogue record for this book is available from the British Library.

Printed and bound in the UK by TJ International, Padstow, Cornwall
Typeset in 11pt Aldine401 BT Roman by Troubador Publishing Ltd, Leicester, UK

Matador is an imprint of Troubador Publishing Ltd

MIX
Paper from
responsible sources
FSC® C013056

*To Antoinette
who was left behind
and who was there when I got back*

FOREWORD

The Gulf War, fought over twenty years ago, is simultaneously still close to us and yet somehow remote. Its proximity is easily explained. The war was, in the eyes of many, unfinished. Saddam Hussein remained in power, and – we now know – saw the fact that the allies had not toppled him as evidence both of his own invincibility and of his enemies' moral cowardice. That, of course, was not how it was seen in the West, or in the headquarters of General Sir Peter de la Billière, the commander of British forces in the Middle East. The Baathist regime was fighting for its survival; the allied coalition set out to liberate Kuwait, a much more limited aim and one which it achieved in short order. By going in hard from the outset and by sticking to its objectives, the allies seemed to have triumphed. In 1992, General Colin Powell, the chairman of the US Joint Chiefs of Staff, enunciated what has come to be called the "Powell doctrine". The United States, he argued, should only commit its forces when it was prepared to use overwhelming force, when it had the support of the American people, and when it could see a clear exit strategy. Military historians tend to interpret the doctrine as the product of the American experience in Vietnam, reasonably enough as Powell served there, but it can also be seen as embodying the lessons which Powell learnt from the war against Iraq in 1990-1.

Now the Powell doctrine looks battered. The United States returned to Iraq in 2003, and in the initial invasion swept all before it, just as it had done in 1991. However, the initial force was not strong enough to deliver on its wider objectives, the occupation of Iraq, the purging of its government, and the installation of a new elite. Powell, then Secretary of State, was increasingly marginalised within the Bush administration. The United States found itself without a clear exit strategy, and the doctrine became evidence more of exceptionalism in war's conduct rather than of a new norm. It is now rarely referred to. It has become an artefact, a reflection of the moment when the United States enjoyed its unipolar moment of world power, a status which many today see as dissipated not only in the second Gulf War but also in Afghanistan.

Americans do not figure much in Stuart Crawford's amusing, often irreverent, and sometimes politically incorrect memoir. As a staff officer in the British headquarters, he had to give General de la Billière, frequently still attired in his dressing gown and slippers, early morning briefings on how the situation had developed overnight. He records the collective revulsion felt within the headquarters when civilians were killed or when the deaths of military personnel became disproportionate. This reached its peak along the so-called "Highway of Death", the road linking Kuwait City with Iraq, which was littered with the shattered remnants of the retreating Iraqi army. Crawford's horror at killing for the sake of killing was shared by others much more senior to him, including Powell, and led directly to the cease fire which ended the war.

And this is where the war seems remote. The concern to use force with discrimination looks very modern, and is reflected in the best of current counter-insurgency practice. But this was not a counter-insurgency war; this was a war of overwhelming air power (in its first phase) and then manoeuvre by armoured divisions advancing at pace, and commanded by corps headquarters. This was the first and last hurrah of a style of warfare developed to fight the Soviet Union along the inner German border. However, that was not how it was seen at the time. Instead it was taken as evidence that NATO had cracked the conundrum of the operational level of war, and that that approach would have universal application in all wars. It may be too easy to scoff now. After all, there was indeed a straight evolutionary line from the successes of 1991 to those achieved in the initial invasion of 2003. But from the perspective of 2014, the British army in which Stuart Crawford served, like that of the United States, looks light years away from that of today. It possessed skills which today's army has lost just as it has acquired ones its predecessor lacked.

We must be wary of nostalgia. *Sending My Laundry Forward* questions the notion that the British army had reached some sort of acme of professional excellence in 1990-1. It records how slow and ponderous the British advance was by comparison with that of the United States' forces. The army had trained for warfare in Europe against a potential enemy who possessed superior strength in almost every index of conventional equipment, and only a decade earlier it had prepared solely for a dogged defensive battle in the suburbanised landscape of northern Germany. Stuart Crawford records his Regiment's grief as its Chieftain tanks were stripped of the engines which their crews had so lovingly maintained in order to fit out a single British armoured brigade. The "urgent operational requirements" put in place to plug gaps in capability were often not met before the war was over. As the British armed forces are reduced in size in consequence of the 2010 Strategic Defence and Security Review, here is an object lesson in the challenges of force regeneration at short notice. Moreover, although the British army took the first Gulf War as a pointer to a new doctrinal dawn, its political masters clearly saw it as a one-off. "Options for Change", the Conservative defence review designed to cash in the post-Cold War dividend, meant that the 4th Royal Tank Regiment, the unit which Stuart Crawford left to go to war, was disbanded within months of his return. Today there are not four Royal Tank Regiments but only one; that is the measure of how this story captures a past that is within the lifetimes of officers still serving, but which is now increasingly distant.

Reflections on how *Sending My Laundry Forward* affects our understanding of change must be matched by an awareness of how it also illuminates continuity in war. Stuart Crawford's determination to sort out the creature comforts of campaigning mirrors a preoccupation shared by professional soldiers across the ages. Many staff officers of earlier generations would recognise too the partial nature of the knowledge possessed even by supposedly omniscient command organisations. Fewer had the good fortune to serve

A Staff Officer's Account of the First Gulf War

in a war that proved so short and so relatively casualty-free, and also got back home to their new wife in such short order. All of those factors may be reasons why British memoirs of the first Gulf War are so scarce. Stuart Crawford has filled a big gap, and done so with humour and not a little style.

Professor Sir Hew Strachan,
Chichele Professor on the History of War,
Oxford University, and Fellow of All Souls College.

First Gulf War
Theatre of Operations

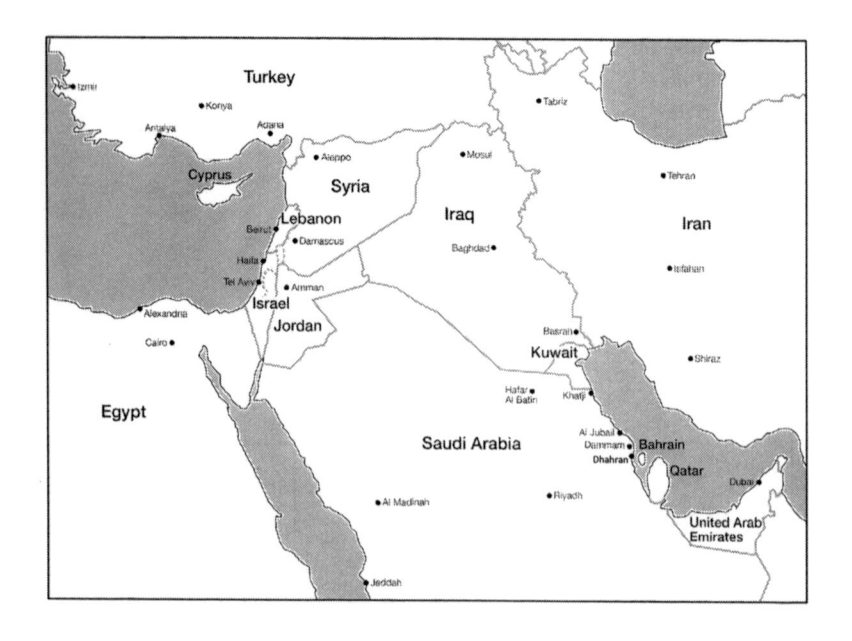

PART 1

Before the Storm

CHAPTER I

Friday 22 November 1990 was a momentous day on two counts. By far and away the most celebrated event, in both senses of the phrase, was the removal of Mrs Thatcher from power by her erstwhile colleagues. Less newsworthy as far as the rest of the world was concerned, but of infinitely more interest to me, was the first inkling that I was likely to be posted to the Gulf as part of that ever growing band of men whose task it might be to wrest back Kuwait from the clutches of Saddam Hussein.

While I am sure that I joined in the collective sigh of relief which swept Britain on the demise of the Prime Minister, my participation was only fleeting, overshadowed by the more personal news. My imminent departure for Saudi Arabia was hardly welcome. I had been married only twelve days before and had rather hoped that my wife Antoinette's introduction to service life was going to be a somewhat gentler affair. The breaker of the news, Colonel John Woodward, then the Regimental Colonel of the Royal Tank Regiment, was probably rather disappointed at my reaction. I told him that it was indeed professionally flattering to be chosen to join the staff of the Headquarters British Forces Middle East (HQBFME) but disastrous as far as my personal life was concerned. I suspect I was meant to be rather more enthusiastic at the prospect of going "on operations."

There was to be no escape, however, and not long thereafter I found myself Gulf bound on an RAF Tristar, having left my bride in Germany in our new house with directions how to get to the NAAFI[1], how to get money out of the bank, and not much else. Typically, my transport picked me up at 3.45 am, not the best time from a psychological point of view to abandon your loved one in the middle of a strange country and go off to war. As I sat amongst my new comrades and baggage on their way to Saudi Arabia, I reflected on how little I knew of what was going on and my part in it. It was only later that I realised that, compared to many of my colleagues, I was very well briefed indeed.

★ ★ ★ ★ ★

Rather like the rest of the world, I suspect, we had been both surprised and not that interested when Iraq invaded and overran Kuwait on 2 August 1990. C and D Squadrons of the 4th Royal Tank Regiment (4RTR), stationed in Imphal Barracks, Osnabruck, were two weeks off deploying to the British Army Training Unit, Suffield, in Canada (always referred to as BATUS) for our biennial training period familiar to all armoured units in British Army of the Rhine at that time. C Squadron, which I commanded, had spent most of the previous year on UN duties in Cyprus in an infantry role, and was firmly focussed on polishing its tank gunnery skills before putting them into practice with live ammunition on the open plains of Alberta. We all had other things on our minds, and apart from a little lighthearted speculation on what might happen next we spent very little time considering the arising problem in the Middle East. We all expected that, if British troops were to become involved at all, our participation would be a replay of the Falklands with 5 Airborne and 3 Commando Brigades being deployed. Our battlegroup[2] going to Canada actually included a company from the 2nd Battalion The Parachute Regiment, but we didn't really expect them to join us now that the Gulf crisis had arisen.

BATUS was, and is, a remarkable training facility which the British army has used under licence from the Canadian government since 1972. It comprises some thousand square miles of prairie in Alberta in western Canada where, because of lack of population, buildings and infrastructure, we were free to manoeuvre and fire our weapons almost at will. For a tank squadron leader and his command it is the final confirmation and testing of competence, a rite of passage between enthusiastic amateur and professional if you like, where every aspect of military skill is applied to a variety of problems set by the staff permanently based there. It is also a hurdle at which many commanders and regiments have fallen over the years and, while officially no report is produced to anyone apart from the commanding officers of units who go there, the word soon gets out when units and individuals are found wanting.

The Canadian prairie is, somewhat paradoxically, both bleak and beautiful. The initial impression of neverending flatness and loneliness is soon replaced by delight at the fascinating folds and rises of the land; far from being flat, the prairie is crossed by numerous riverbeds, called coullees in this part of the world, and broken by hills and escarpments which hide undiscovered valleys and plains. Most of it is wild grassland, which supports a wide array of wildlife from occasional herds of wild mustangs down to the numerous colonies of gophers, some of which are half tame after being fed by visiting troops over the years. There is also evidence of man's previous occupation of the area in the form of stone rings marking where the native Indians pitched their tepees, usually found in the more sheltered sites or near the rivers.

We spent almost exactly a month in Canada, including seventeen days continuously on the prairie living off our tanks. During this time we were almost oblivious to the deepening crisis in the Middle East, although we knew that some of the Paras had been kept back in Aldershot in case of a rapid deployment. The training was hot, hard, and sometimes mind-numbingly exhausting, but on occasions quite overwhelmingly exhilerating. At the end we felt that we had acquitted ourselves well and were "ready for role".

On the second day of our return to the relatively civilised environment of Camp Crowfoot, a collection of prefabricated huts on the edge of the training area, the news reached us that 7 Armoured Brigade was being deployed to the Gulf. This was met with disappointment by some and relief by others; had 12 Armoured Brigade been chosen, then we ourselves would have been on our way. The consensus amongst the officers was that we had no desire to be gassed or have our heads blown off on account of some mad tinpot dictator in an area of the world that had little relevance as far as we could see. Let others go, and good luck to them. Little did we realise that back in Osnabruck the OC Rear Party, Peter Loggie, was already being ordered to find 4RTR personnel to augment 7 Armoured Brigade and that some of the younger officers were falling over themselves to volunteer. When Alistair Fyfe, commanding D Squadron, and I discovered this we discussed the phenomenon at length and agreed that being sent was one thing but volunteering quite another, and that both of us would wait for the former!

On return to Germany I gave up command of C Squadron and took up my new appointment of Regimental Second-in-Command (2IC). I had been at my desk in Regimental Headquarters for only a morning and was still in the middle of taking over the job from my predecessor when, with no notice, the first batch of REME[3] tradesmen descended on the Regiment to strip our Chieftain tanks for spares. The Commanding Officer, Lt Col Charlie McBean, was not the type of man to take this sort of thing lying down but, after a couple of fairly heated phone calls, even he had to stand aside. Thus, at a stroke, 4RTR was rendered non-operational and we were not to see our tanks whole again until many months after our colleagues returned from the Gulf. In the end, we provided amongst other things forty Chieftain gearboxes, thirteen engines, ten gun barrels, and a host of other pieces of automotive and gunnery equipment. Our Reconnaissance Troop had engines and gearboxes stripped from all of its eight Scorpion vehicles. Particularly annoying to the tank crews who had nurtured their vehicles with pride over the years was the hasty and unprofessional way in which some of the stripping was carried out. In some cases the REME had cut expensive cables to remove items to save time and trouble in unscrewing them. When the scavengers finally left we had not one of our fifty-seven tanks serviceable.

From this point onwards, really, we became an Operation Granby (as the British operation had by now been christened) support Regiment. Over the next few months we provided assistance in many forms. We despatched paint teams to 7 Armoured Brigade units to help prepare their vehicles. We lent out all our NBC[4] instructors to help train personnel in the face of the very real threat of the Iraqis using chemical and biological weapons. We also had to provide a number of soldiers as Battle Casualty Replacements (BCRs), men who were to deploy to the area of operations but be kept in reserve until sent forward to replace those killed and wounded in action.[5] Initially, all BCRs were volunteers, but eventually they dried up. I can well remember the OC G Squadron, Ron Aqualina, coming in to report that he was short of two volunteers to fill a particular BCR quota. I had to advise him that he would therefore need to order a couple of soldiers to fulfil the task, which he duly did. To their credit, the men concerned complied without a murmur as good soldiers should, their only concern being how to break the news to their wives. A lot of soldiers were keen enough to go but were under strict orders from their spouses not even to think of volunteering![6]

By this point life in Imphal Barracks, Osnabruck was becoming extremely unpredictable. Regimental taskings seemed to change hourly and we began to suspect that much we were being asked to do at short notice was because of "knee jerk" reactions in various places. It appeared as if nobody was really coordinating the vast amount of effort being made to prepare the Brigade for the Gulf. One of my jobs as Regimental 2IC was to oversee the production of the annual forecast of events, but this task was given up as hopeless very early in the proceedings. One day we were stoodby to go to Northern Ireland, the next we were tasked to send squadrons to both the Gulf and Berlin. Eventually we were excited by nothing until it actually happened and took each day as it came.

Meanwhile the soldiers we had "exported" to assist various other organisations preparing to deploy came home at the weekends and told us what was happening elsewhere. It wasn't particularly reassuring as far as the overall competence of 7 Armoured Brigade in general, and the Royal Armoured Corps units in it in particular, were concerned. Some of the Brigade units were by all accounts pretty poorly trained at this point. We learned that the Queen's Royal Irish Hussars[7] were, in the opinion of our young officers who were working with them, so "awful" that to a man they politely declined offers of employment in the Middle East with them despite being desperately keen to go. Those attached to the Royal Scots Dragoon Guards, a particularly fine Regiment, were taken aback by how poorly versed in individual skills their soldiers proved to be, comparing them unfavourably with new recruits straight out of training. Of course, a certain amount of this can be put down to Regimental pride and bravado, but at the time there was a definite undercurrent of doubt as to just how good some of these organisations were.

SENDING MY LAUNDRY FORWARD

Those of us not directly involved in preparations for deployment felt a little like bystanders while 7 Brigade worked itself up for deployment. Our work in support of Op Granby, time consuming though it was, constituted a small part of 4RTR's daily activities. Despite our equipment being inoperable and many of our personnel seconded elsewhere, the whole spectrum of normal peacetime soldiering tasks remained, and we spent most of our time and effort doing the sort of things we always did. For my part I was deeply involved in financial matters relating to the amalgamations within the Royal Tank Regiment which we knew were bound to happen, Gulf crisis or no. Elsewhere promotion conferences were being run, and of course there was no let up in anti terrorist security measures with concomitant large daily manpower bill. To say we were overworked would be an exaggeration, but there wasn't much slack left in the system. Round about the same time we had a change of Commanding Officer, with Lt Col Martin Speller replacing Charles McBean. Colonel Charlie's leaving was a splendid affair, with most of the Regimental silver on display and the dining room nicely decorated with flowers by the wives. The Pipes and Drums played magnificently throughout the evening and it was a most fitting occasion for the end of the CO's tour.

It was now the end of October, and things were moving on apace in the Middle East. Our first soldiers deployed to the Gulf during the last days of the month as part of the BCR contingent, and meanwhile the first elements of 7 Armoured Brigade had begun to arrive at the port of Al Jubail in Saudi Arabia. Television was full of Challenger tanks painted in their new desert colours unloading, and Saddam Hussein reportedly put his army on alert for an American attack. Back home in Britain, hospitals were told to standby for casualties from four days after November 16 – bluff or truth we knew not. It all seemed to have become much more serious somehow. Against this rather sombre background I went on leave to get married on November 10.

★ ★ ★ ★ ★

I returned to work in Germany from honeymoon for only one day before flying back to Bovington[8] to find that everything as far as the Regiment was concerned had changed yet again. Our one squadron commitment to Op Granby had been stood down, much to the relief, I suspect, of Alistair Fyfe who was down to command it. During my absence the British commitment had risen to a Division, although a fairly weak one, and 4 Armoured Brigade and HQ 1 Armoured Division were now preparing to join 7 Armoured Brigade in Saudi Arabia. It being 20 November and a Regimental holiday[9], I joined the Adjutant, Pablo Miller, in serenading the CO in his quarter with the complete Pipes and Drums at 6.45 in the morning. As always this was greeted stoically by the CO who responded with tea and whisky – "gunfire", as it's called – and sent us on our slightly intoxicated way to pay the same early morning call to the boys in the barrack blocks. You need an iron constitution to survive days like this and I was not too disappointed to extract myself from the festivities early on and catch a 'plane to England to attend the RTR 2IC's conference at Bovington.

It was during this conference that I first heard I was being considered for a post in the HQBFME, which came as a complete surprise. I had thought that, being 2IC of the Regiment and therefore very much part of the fabric, it was most unlikely that I would be extracted and sent to the Gulf. According to the Regimental Colonel they needed a man with Armoured Corps experience out there, and the technical qualifications I had stood me in good stead to assist with the urgent programme of equipment modifications and procurement required before the Division joined battle. I rather wondered why, having been told for years that our equipment and weapons were more than a match for anything the Soviets could throw at us, it was necessary to modify and improve these same equipments and weapons before we could face the altogether less sophisticated and competent Iraqis. It did not fill me with great confidence. Neither did being told that the job was in Jeddah, when in fact it turned out to be in Riyadh! I must admit that, despite having made the point quite forcibly that this job in the Gulf was not my idea of a great adventure at this particular juncture, I didn't really expect it to come to anything. I only realised later that, with the Royal Tank Regiment not forming any part of the British force in Saudi Arabia, it was politically imperative to get as many individuals out there as possible to maintain the Regimental profile. Everybody saw the defence cuts coming and wanted as much ammunition to fight their respective corners as possible.

I returned to Germany and for the next couple of days had my hands full trying to curb the excessive enthusiasm of the new CO, Martin Speller. He faced the unenviable task of motivating and inventing a worthwhile programme for a Regiment which had been rendered ineffective in its primary role by the rape of its vehicles and, more and more, its men. No sooner would we design a programme than it would be upset by yet another demand for Op Granby. We were flabbergasted when HQ 1 Armoured Division produced a manpower request which called for an *additional* thirty-two officers to man the HQ. Who had we been kidding by pretending that we had been fully manned and ready for all these years in Germany? Only ourselves, I suspect. Eventually we were forced to recall some of our young officers from courses in Britain to meet the manpower bill.

Finally, during one of the many conferences we held each day at this point, the CO received a 'phone call which confirmed that I was indeed to be posted to HQBFME, no move before 11 December. Having been warned to some extent well in advance, I can't say the news came as any great surprise, nor did it excite me greatly. Professionally it would be interesting to see the theory being translated into practice after ten years or so in the army, but domestically it couldn't have come at a worse time with Antoinette having spent only four days in Germany in our new house. Nevertheless, one gets rather used to such turns of event in the army and I suppose I was fairly philosophical about it. The CO was very good about it all and I was told to hand over the job that I had barely taken over myself and then go on leave until my deployment date. I didn't need a second bidding and did just that. Just before leaving for Britain, and having had yellow fever and cholera injections from the TA doctors who had relieved the regulars who were already in Saudi Arabia, I received a signal informing me that I was to deploy to the Gulf on 19 December.

PART 2

The Clouds Gather

CHAPTER II

At 3.45 am on the cold and bleak morning of 19 December the CO's staff car driver, Lance Corporal Twigger, arrived at my front door to drive me to RAF Wildenrath. The army always instigates such trips at unearthly hours, and thus I started my journey to war on a psychological low. Although naturally concerned for my wellbeing, my parents had been fairly matter-of-fact over my departure for the Gulf, realising that I was comparatively lucky and safe from the as yet unknown dangers by virtue of my posting to the theatre HQ, which was hardly the front line. For Antoinette it was less easily accepted, and although she was very brave about it my leaving was not exactly a joyous occasion. I found myself wondering how it was for all those young men who set off in similar circumstances in 1914 and 1939, many of whom were never heard of or seen again by their wives and families. At least mine would hear of me again, for I doubted that Saudi Arabia would be totally devoid of telephones, and I counted myself relatively fortunate.

LCpl Twigger made a good job of getting me to Wildenrath for the flight, and I had a few moments to spare before boarding. Here was my first sighting in the flesh of soldiers in desert uniform, sported by those who had been lucky enough to get sent back to Germany for a few days' leave. The flight staged through Brize Norton in Oxfordshire, where we had a short break before embarking once more for Riyadh. At this point I met Tony Russ, a Royal Signals officer who had attended the same Camberley course as I[10], and also Charlie Wiggin, a Grenadier Guardsman who was destined for HQBFME. They had as little idea of what was going on as I did, but my knowledge of what lay in store increased tenfold when Brigadier Philip Sanders, who had been CO of 4RTR when I was a Lieutenant and whom I knew well, told me in outline what was expected of me. He was working at Joint Headquarters High Wycombe[11], from where Op Granby was being directed, and had been partly instrumental in me getting the job. From him, sitting in the aisle of the Tristar, I learnt that I was likely to join the night shift staff which formed part of the twenty-four hour manning requirement should hostilities break out.

I was also both surprised and amused to see Paul Daniels, the well known magician and television personality, on the same flight, on his way to the Gulf to entertain the troops. The media had latched on to the fact that British servicemen would be away from home over Christmas and New Year and a number of showbusiness personalities had volunteered to go out to cheer up the boys over the holiday period. To be honest, I had never been an avid fan of Mr Daniels even though I recognised his skill and talent. What I was not prepared for, however, was the ease with which he mixed with the soldiers on the flight and whose rapt attention he very quickly gained. He walked back from the front of the aircraft, where VIPs are habitually placed in the marginally more comfortable seats, and within five minutes or so had most of the aircraft laughing and baffled by his tricks. He was particularly amusing during our unscheduled refuelling stop in Cairo, although regrettably I can't remember what he said. He certainly cheered up our little trip into the unknown and went up in my estimation considerably.

Eventually we landed at King Khaled Airport, Riyadh, at two o'clock in the morning. On deplaning, my first impression was that I had strayed into some Hollywood film lot, full of half completed buildings and facades. It was rather like entering Batman's Gotham City, with piercing arc lights alternating with deep shadows where transport 'planes and equipment of all shapes and sizes lurked. The reality was that the airport was only half constructed but had been pressed into service to cope with the exigencies of the situation. The Royal Engineers had put up a few dividing walls and ablutions in an attempt to make the place habitable, but it remained a grim and depressing place. I was glad to see Ian Rodley, 1st Royal Tank Regiment, and Richard Aubrey-Fletcher, Grenadier Guards, both of whom I knew from Staff College, who had come to collect us. They were both veterans, having arrived a week earlier, and we in our abject ignorance of what was going on latched on to their every word. On the way into Riyadh we learnt to our astonishment that we were to be accommodated in the Riyadh Marriot Hotel free of charge *and* receive £41 per day to pay for food, all on top of our normal pay. Ian commented that it was a bit like being in GHQ[12] in a chateau in 1914, and he wasn't too far off the mark. Brigadier Sanders told me I'd be thoroughly bored of it within a fortnight; I didn't believe him, of course, but he was right.

SENDING MY LAUNDRY FORWARD

As a new boy just arrived "in theatre", I was allowed a lie in on the following day. I treated myself to breakfast in my room, went downstairs (or more accurately, downlift – this being an American style hotel) for a coffee, and sent a fax to 4RTR to let them and Antoinette know I had arrived. I was then picked up and taken to HQBFME, a rather grand title for what was at this stage an organisation rapidly expanding from its usual peacetime size and housed rather ingloriously in a couple of fairly mediocre commercial office blocks. My feeling after a quick tour of the setup was of something rather embryonic and nebulous, all rather disjointed and lacking clear direction. This was reinforced when I reported to the Chief of Staff (COS) of the Land Cell[13], Colonel Ian Talbot, who asked me in a friendly way what I was doing out there and what job I was meant to fill! So much for all the nonsense I had been fed by Regiment and personnel branch about being the right man for the job, specially selected, and so forth. He informed me that I was to assist Lt Col James Short who was almost singlehandedly running the equipment upgrade and procurement side of life and was in danger of being overwhelmed. He was also away at the time, so I was a spare body in the short term. Having sorted a desk out for myself – those arriving earlier had to screw their own desks together and go out and buy stationery from the local shops – I drew my first batch of allowances from the Paymaster. This was to last me to the end of the month and amounted to nearly £540. A little ritual had been established by then which I had been advised to follow; from the Paymaster's office you went directly across the yard to the British Forces Post Office in the next portacabin, where you deposited the bulk of the money in a Post Office Investment Account. The allowances far exceeded our requirements and most people were making considerable savings, much to the irritation of the boys in the desert who lived out in the open and got very little at all.[14]

The slight feeling of unreality was further reinforced when we went to collect our staff cars – two brand spanking new Mazda 929s courtesy of the Saudi government, so we were told. Mine had twenty-three miles on the clock. There seemed to be a bottomless pit of money and resources, and it appeared at first that if you wanted anything the Quartermaster went out and bought it. I found the whole experience rather disconcerting, as if nothing was really properly tied down and nobody was really in charge. When the outline planning began I felt very much as if I was involved in another Staff College exercise, which is either a compliment to the realism of Staff College training or a criticism that it too is rather nebulous and ill defined. I never did make up my mind which was more accurate. However, the first day finished on a little high note with the distribution of the Red Cross/Daily Telegraph parcel, one per man. These contained a number of things like toothpaste, shaving soap, a torch, a frisbee, and so on and were great for morale. A big pallet of these parcels stood in the yard outside HQBFME for a couple of weeks before being sent up country but to my knowledge nobody took more than one, although there were rumours of pilfering by the locals.

The next day started in dramatic fashion. It was a Friday, the Saudi equivalent to Sunday, so we had arranged a leisurely start and arrived at work at about 1030 am. As we did so, with me proudly driving my Mazda 929, we noticed people flying about all over the place with serious expresssions. It turned out to be the first of our many SCUD[15] alerts, and people were feverishly getting into their NBC suits in case of chemical or biological attack. We were stood down fairly rapidly, and were informed later that it had in fact been as a result of the Israelis doing some practice firing of their "Jericho" missiles into the Mediterranean. No doubt there was a message for somebody there. I made a mental note to enrol myself in the NBC refresher classes which were run every lunchtime in the yard; my knowledge of such matters was a little rusty and I was in need of some revision. That morning we also heard the very sad news that Andrew Burch, a REME officer working in the HQ and yet another from my year at Staff College, had been killed in a car crash the night before while driving up country. Ian Rodley had been called out in the middle of the night to carry out the unpleasant task of identifying the body. We understood that his car had been hit by a lorry driven by an illegal immigrant with no licence or insurance, and rumour later had it that the other driver had been shot by the Saudi police. I think we were all rather shocked, but we never found out if this was in fact true.

The first few days were taken up with getting to grips with the vast number of Urgent Operational Requirements (UORs) which had arisen. These were documents in a more or less standard form which presented the cases for a huge array of equipment requirements, either modifications or totally new items, deemed necessary for the impending war. They ranged from uparmouring kits for the Challenger tanks and Warrior infantry fighting vehicles right down to "knobbly" tyres for motorcycles to improve traction in the sand. Every branch seemed to be using the opportunity to fulfil its long term equipment aspirations, and large sums of money were sometimes being expended on equipment of dubious utility as various hobby horses were exercised. Again, there appeared to be little central control, and up to this point Lt Col James Short had been running a one man show in theatre. It was obvious that, should anything happen to him, we would be lost and so, with his agreement, we began to create a filing and record system which brought a little order to the administration. I also met the US Army in Saudi for the first time when with Ian Rodley I visited CENTCOM[16], situated just down the road from us in Riyadh in the Saudi Ministry of Defence (MOD). We were mildly surprised at the lax attitude to security shown by the Saudi guards; it appeared that anybody who looked the least bit important was let in without showing any sort of pass. The building itself was magnificent, however, and put our own MOD in Whitehall to shame.

On 23 December I drove to Al Jubail to visit HQ 1 Armoured Division. As expected, the port area was staggeringly busy. There were acres of crates, rows of tanks, helicopters, and other military vehicles, and more military activity than I had ever seen before. At the Divisional HQ I met Duncan MacMillan and Dave Cowan, both from my own Regiment and seconded as watchkeepers to Division. They were both in good spirits and working long hours, although much of it was spent hanging around waiting for something to happen. I was there to attend a meeting on

Challenger and Warrior modifications at which the GOC[17], General Rupert Smith, was present. I had never seen him before but thought he looked very tired. There was much concern about the reliability of Challenger, with one breaking down every five to six kilometres on route marches. There was a certain amount of worry that the Division would not be ready by 31 January 1991, a date which meant nothing to me, although I knew they planned to deploy into the desert around 5 January.

Somewhat surprisingly to those of us in Saudi, it became increasingly difficult for us to achieve much on the equipment front because most of the agencies we dealt with in Britain closed for Christmas. We intended to work throughout, as did the Division in Al Jubail, but on reduced manning to allow a modicum of relaxation. Troops and equipment were arriving in theatre every hour and there was much to be done. But despite the news reports which were becoming ever more gloomy we still expected that the crisis would be resolved peacefully. Saddam Hussein, we speculated, would allow us all to deploy to the Gulf, take it to the brink of war, and then withdraw from Kuwait leaving us all feeling rather foolish.

And so Christmas Day arrived. My name had not appeared on the work roster, but I went in anyway as there wasn't much else to do. Both MOD and JHQ High Wycombe were on skeleton manning so there was little activity. In the afternoon Ian Rodley and I went off to the Diplomatic Quarter as we had very kindly been invited to Christmas lunch by Charles Hollis, one of the British diplomats. This was a very jolly affair, complete with turkey, roast potatoes, and even real beer and wine, which of course was not allowed under Saudi law outside the diplomatic compound. A very nice New Zealand couple who were also there had bought us some Christmas presents, which was very touching, and for a little while we were transported back to normality. The alcohol went straight to our heads for we had been teetotal up to that point, but we drove back anyway, reasoning that a country which did not allow any alcohol wouldn't have any need for drink driving laws and we would therefore be quite legal! I don't think any of us would have chosen to spend Christmas thus, but in the circumstances it was most agreeable and we were very grateful that people looked after us so well.

The few days following Christmas were generally quiet in the HQ. There were a couple of SCUD alerts which lasted just long enough for people to struggle into their NBC kit before being cancelled. It also became clear that, having ordered large amounts of equipment to be delivered with all possible speed to Saudi Arabia, no-one quite knew how or when it might arrive. There was a disconnect between those sending the kit, those actually loading it, and those receiving it, and on a number of occasions we were clamouring for particular items to be sent out on the next available ship or 'plane when the bits in question had already been delivered. This problem never went away during the course of the crisis, and a large amount of equipment was not located in time for use. Perhaps the best example of this was the fact that we never knew for sure exactly how many Challenger tanks were in theatre. We knew how many *should* have been there, but were never able to prove that some helpful individual hadn't squeezed an extra one on a ship with some spare room. The only way we could have been 100% sure of tank numbers would have been to have lined them all up in one place and counted them, which was of course out of the question. Making war is not an exact science, a lesson which was reinforced many times as Op Granby unfolded.

During this period the Chief of the General Staff, General Sir John Chapple, visited HQBFME with a small entourage. We were already becoming a little cynical of the large numbers of extraneous individuals who were arriving in theatre to try and get in on the action, but of course CGS had every right to be there and it was entirely appropriate that he visit the Gulf at this time. He didn't make a particularly favourable impact on us, but he seemed jolly enough. Unfortunately, some idiot had kitted him out in desert combat uniform, no doubt thinking that CGS should appear before his troops in the correct garb. What he probably didn't realise, however, was that such uniforms were in extremely short supply; we certainly hadn't been issued with any, nor had the majority of the boys in the desert. Desert uniform, or more specifically the lack of it, was a particularly sensitive matter throughout the war and CGS and his followers did themselves no favours by appearing in it when those who really needed it were still doing without. Little matters like this take on a whole new significance in times of stress, and really CGS should have known better. The subject was much more sensitively handled by the Colonel in charge of supply in HQBFME, who steadfastly refused to don desert combats until he was sure every soldier in theatre had at least one set.

He stuck to his guns, and did not kit himself out until well into the war.

A few days before New Year all the newcomers, including myself, were briefed by the Commander BFME, General Sir Peter de la Billière, in whose HQ we were working. I had seen him a number of times before, but always at a distance, and so was most interested to see and hear him in the relative intimacy of his office. He spoke rather amiably to us all for quite some time about the situation in general but didn't tell us anything dramatic. I remember being amazed at the geographical span of his command, stretching as it did some way beyond the borders of Saudi Arabia and Kuwait and encompassing all three Services' areas of operation. He invited questions from us after his briefing and answered them all, although he refused to be drawn on whether the Iraqi use of chemical weapons would elicit a nuclear response. We all guessed it would, but were left none the wiser. I left the office with the impression of a quietly spoken and likeable individual who was facing a rather daunting task with some relish. Some people were to say later that he was past his sell by date and the job would be better done by a younger man, but nothing I saw persuaded me that this was the case. I was to see the General – "DLB" as he was usually referred to – a little more regularly when war broke out.

I kept bumping into people I knew in Riyadh, and it seemed sometimes as if most of the British army was in Saudi Arabia. Jonathan Campbell-James, yet another Staff College friend, had been ensconced in the Diplomatic Quarter for some time and was always able to offer a beer, usually under protest, if we wanted to escape for a few hours. I also met my old Sandhurst chum, Howard Hughes, who was running the Royal Engineers Postal Services and whom I hadn't seen since 1981. He told me that the BFPOs were handling £250,000 a week through Post Office and National Savings Accounts which had been opened by those receiving allowances.

At about this time the newspapers became noticeably more pessimistic about the chances of a peaceful solution to the crisis. Jordan was reported to have moved two brigades up to the Israeli border, and there were continuing hints that there was a very real biological warfare (BW) threat as well as a chemical one. This was confirmed when we were told that inoculations against anthrax and whooping cough were to be made available to those who wished them. Nobody was particularly surprised. There was a lighter side to life as well, however, and I laughed heartily at the directions I was given by my colleagues when I had to pick up a visitor from Britain: "Down to Suicide Roundabout[18], left to the Coffee Pot, left again and straight on until you see the Two SCUDS[19], left again down to the Sheraton and you can't miss it." The Gulf expedition was already creating a jargon of its own, some of which had already appeared in the British press.

In such a fashion 1990 passed away rather quietly, with no New Year celebrations in Riyadh of which I was aware. I think many of us in HQBFME felt a bit lonely at this point; there was none of the festivity of Christmas and we were a long way from home. Although we all got on very well, we did not yet have any semblance of the camaraderie and esprit de corps which is found in a battalion or regiment. To all intents and purpose we were a scratch organisation trying desperately to catch up with events. We therefore had little time to devote to the more complex human and emotional aspects of being uprooted and sent to a strange country to work in a strange environment with strange people. There was often a feeling of being unable to control events and one's own destiny, of being caught up in circumstances where one's fate could be decided by the whim of another. In my own case, I had hardly arrived in Riyadh and found my desk when I was told not to unpack as I might be sent forward to Divisional HQ, only to be told to forget it two hours later. All of this was very unsettling, and we became very wary of people with "good ideas."

Nevertheless, the end of the year found us in reasonably good spirits and beginning to get on top of the work. We realised that the chances of resolving the crisis without going to war were slipping away, but still held out hope that common sense would win the day. But with nearly 430,000 US troops in Saudi Arabia and Saddam Hussein vowing he would attack Israel if the UN Resolution was carried out it seemed that there was little room for manoeuvre left. As far as our personal security was concerned, the arrival of a company of the Queen's Own Highlanders to guard the HQ put our minds at ease, for we had been terribly vulnerable to terrorist attack up to that point. Their soft Highland lilts and friendly but guttural Glasgow patois also took the edge off my homesickness, and with a certain amount of excitement and optimism we looked forward to see what the New Year would bring.

CHAPTER III

The New Year was nearly a very short one for me. Travelling down the motorway to Al Jubail with Chris Coomber, a civilian scientist from the Royal Armaments Research and Development Establishment (RARDE)[20], we suffered a blow out at 100mph. Chris was driving and controlled it very well, aided by the fact there was no other traffic on the road, but it shook us up a bit and made us late for our rendezvous with Major John Cantwell, an Australian officer from the Royal Australian Armoured Corps who was on attachment to HQ 1 Armoured Division in Germany when it was warned for the Gulf. He was rather proud of the fact that his presence in Saudi on operations with the British army had been specifically approved by the Australian government – " licenced to die", as he put it – and he now found himself in charge of the Challenger uparmouring programme. He drove us out in his Range Rover, one of the many hired to supplement existing vehicle stocks, to the alliteratively named Devil Dog Dragoon Range on the Gulf coast. Here the Royal Scots Dragoon Guards were conducting firing trials on their Challengers, including firing some of the new depleted uranium (DU) rounds which they weren't really supposed to at that time. The firing was being directed by Captain Albert Hogg, one of the

RAC's gunnery experts and an old acquaintance, and I was delighted to meet Sergeant Jimmy Simpson from 4RTR, who was serving as a troop sergeant in A Squadron of the Dragoon Guards. He and I had known each other since I joined the army and he had recently been one of my troop sergeants in C Squadron 4RTR. He was always an amusing individual and I enjoyed listening to his banter for a moment or two in that rather odd environment.

On the way back to Divisional HQ in Al Jubail I was once again reminded of the scale of effort involved in mounting this operation. The desert was quite literally *covered* by vehicles of all descriptions, either moving cross country or stationary and camouflaged under nets. The main road north from the ports of Al Jubail, Dammam, and Dhahran was one continuous stream of American equipment which completely filled the inside lane of the motorway without a break. There was still some civilian traffic, but it was outnumbered many times by the vast numbers of military vehicles.

On reaching HQ 1 Armoured Division, still located in transit accommodation on the outskirts of Jubail, I did my round of the desks to see what needed to be done back in Riyadh before going to the temporary cookhouse for supper. I noted on my way that being on operations had already led to a certain relaxation in dress discipline – the sentry stood resplendent in American slouch hat, temperate climate combat jacket, desert pattern combat trousers, desert boots, and a pink shamagh round his neck. Such a combination would have been unthinkable back in Germany a couple of weeks earlier, but the British army has a long history of going slightly peculiar in desert environments stretching back beyond T E Lawrence. The sentry was continuing this tradition, and indeed the GOC walked past him two minutes later without even a sniff of disapproval.

I was also mightily impressed to note that General Smith and his companions joined the queue for dinner behind some private soldiers and waited their turn to be served, and on getting their food sat down amongst the troops. Not unusual, you might think, in an army where subalterns have long been taught to eat only after their men had been fed, but something happens to officers as they reach the more senior levels. Most other GOCs would have either walked to the head of the queue or been served separately elsewhere, and it restored a little of my faith in the system to see a General who had not lost touch. The meal itself was the usual plain but hearty fare, and afterwards I retired for the night to my room which I shared with six others, including a very glum Warrant Officer who complained bitterly that at his age he shouldn't be on operations and he hadn't joined the army for this sort of thing in the first place!

In the morning Chris Coomber and I headed off to the Forward Mounting Area (FMA) nearer the port area where I dropped him off. The HQ was in the middle of a self imposed NBC exercise when we arrived, so we both had to struggle into full NBC kit before entering the compound where all the in theatre logistic planning for this massive undertaking was being carried out. Everybody looks the same in an NBC mask, so finding the right people in the HQ took some time, but eventually I was back on the road to Riyadh and glad not to have to stay in the chaos of Al Jubail. The wind was quite blustery on the motorway, and sand was being blown from the desert directly across the carriageway. I discovered that the desert is not yellow but pink, although whether that was because of the light at that particular time of day I was never sure. I had always wondered why the SAS in the Second World War in North Africa had painted their vehicles pink, and now I had the answer. It was a bit peculiar but also rather beautiful.

A couple of days later I returned to deliver a party of scientists to Divisional HQ, driving a brand new Land Rover Discovery which I managed to borrow from someone or other. By this time the Division had deployed into the desert, and nobody seemed to know exactly where the HQ was. There were literally hundreds of little groups of camouflaged vehicles all across the desert, and it was impossible to tell which organisation was which from a distance. Eventually, after much to-ing and fro-ing, it was decided to drop the scientists at Divisional Supply Area (DSA)1, an undistinguished little huddle of tents and Land Rovers near the road. I don't think these learned gentlemen were particularly impressed at being abandoned, or indeed by my navigation prowess, but they didn't grumble and were picked up shortly afterwards by our tame Australian, John Cantwell, and taken to their proper destination. This scenario was typical of many occurring at this time, for the situation was still confused and men and material were arriving in Saudi in a seemingly endless stream.

We were vaguely aware of politics back in Britain despite being somewhat isolated by distance and culture, and of course John Major had by this time, a little surprisingly we

SENDING MY LAUNDRY FORWARD

thought, filled the vacated throne left by Margaret Thatcher. The new Prime Minister now visited his troops in the Gulf and by all accounts acquitted himself well in the soldiers' eyes. He arrived at HQBFME on 7 January, but I just couldn't motivate myself to go and listen to his message to us. In retrospect this appears rather arrogant, but at the time I had so much to do that the last thing I needed was to be on the receiving end of a stream of well intentioned platitudes from a man I did not, and still do not, find particularly impressive. On the same day, and much more interesting by far, was the first broadcast on Saudi television instructing the population on actions to be taken in the event of air raid or missile attack. It began to dawn on us all that things were beginning to get a little serious, and that it was probably not physically possible any longer for Iraq to pull out of Kuwait and still comply with the UN deadline. Personally I thought it was all too late, and it was a sobering thought.

Just about this time one of the more intriguing incidents of the pre war period happened, alluded to by General Sir Peter in his book *Storm Command*.[21] We received the news in the HQ that morning that six Iraqi helicopters had crossed the Saudi/Kuwaiti border the night before and had landed in Saudi Arabia. At the time we presumed they were defecting and thought little more of it, but our interest was aroused later that same day when the Saudis denied it had ever happened. There was lots of speculation, of course, and the favourite theory was that it was a covert special forces (SF) operation returning, but we never did find out the true story nor, as I now know, did our Commander!

A welcome relief to the constant paperwork came when

we set about sandbagging the HQ. Many people, my wife included, had already assumed that we were safely ensconced in some concrete bunker out of harm's way. The reality was that at this point we were occupying a rather scruffy office block similar to many others in Riyadh. We were becoming more concerned about terrorist attack than anything else, and so eventually we set to protecting ourselves. I was delighted to escape the fetid atmosphere of our cramped office, roll up my sleeves, and indulge in some honest toil in the warm, spring like weather outside. At the end of the day we had constructed a blast shelter wall outside the entrance, sandbagged all the windows on the ground floor, and covered all the panes of glass with fablon to prevent flying splinters in the event of a bomb attack. I don't think our efforts would have protected us from much more than a hand grenade, but we all felt the better for it. That night I was duty officer and slept overnight in the HQ. I was woken only once, and then only by a member of the RAF who was lost and 'phoned for directions to the airfield!

On 12 January we went on to twenty-four hour manning and I joined the night shift. Things became noticeably more serious at this point; the Americans started wearing helmets and body armour and our Queen's Own Highlander guards were doubly vigilant. We decided to move out of the Marriott Hotel, which was still full of business men and Kuwaiti refugee families, to a smaller compound where we were more secure. Worst of all for many was the news that our allowances were shortly to stop as there were now sufficient personnel in HQBFME to justify the deployment of a catering unit to feed us. The gravy train had thus come to an end, and I think most of us felt that we'd had more than enough of a good thing anyway.[22]

The Land Cell night shift consisted of myself, Richard Aubrey-Fletcher, and Henry Spender, while Ian Rodley, Charlie Wiggin, and Chris Manning AAC covered the day shift. It was a most satisfactory arrangement for most of the time, and a sort of friendly rivalry grew up between us as time progressed. Generally speaking there was very much less to do at night, although we were to have some excitement in the weeks ahead. Working at night was rather strange to begin with, because not everybody went on to twenty-four hour manning at the same time. We all found it extremely difficult to stay awake between 0330 and 0530 on the first night, but slowly our body clocks adjusted. Nothing very much happened in the first couple of nights in any case. The highlight of this time was the arrival of a huge hamper from Antoinette, containing, amongst other things, a pair of swimming trunks and a bottle of port. The former were a result of my boasting that the Marriott had a swimming pool, but unfortunately I'd moved out before they arrived. The latter was most definitely contraband, but most welcome for all that.

Alcohol was strictly verboten in deference to the customs of our Saudi hosts, and the only place that one could legitimately consume it was in the Diplomatic Quarter. However, ever since the first servicemen had arrived in Saudi it had been around. The first I saw in Riyadh was in a shampoo bottle sent to one of my HQBFME colleagues by his wife. Sadly, she had failed to rinse the bottle sufficiently and by all accounts it tasted strongly of Vosene or Head and Shoulders, or whatever brand the bottle formerly carried. It was, nevertheless, consumed. It had been noted early on that parcels were seldom if ever investigated, and from then on there was a constant trickle of bottles in the mail. Almost without exception the lucky recipient shared it around, as did I with my port, and I doubt if anyone had more than a few mouthfuls during their stay. The boys in the desert had it too, and many a hard day's training was rounded off with a wee nip from the bottle stashed in the turret bin. There are those who will attribute the excellent disciplinary record of British troops in Saudi Arabia to the absence of alcohol, and no doubt it was partially the reason, but the fact remains that even if soldiers had been blind drunk there were no bars to fight in, no civilians to annoy, no cars to drive, and no women to chase. Drink or no drink, it just wasn't easy to get into trouble! In any case, the amount of alcohol around was negligible and it didn't make any difference.

More and more of our time began to be taken up answering some rather basic detailed questions from JHQ High Wycombe, the pettiness of which began to irritate us. It was, in retrospect, indicative of how little they had to do and of how left out of the picture they sometimes felt. We tried to explain that there wasn't very much at all going on in Saudi Arabia, but they never quite believed us and always thought we were hiding something. One night I was taken to task for not reporting the discovery of one RPG7[23] on the beach south of Al Jubail, a matter which would not normally rate more than a mention in a battalion's daily intelligence report, but such was the thirst for information, any information, back at JHQ that it became the object of intense interest for a while. Did it mean that Iraqi special forces had landed behind us and were about to wreak havoc in our rear areas? We never found out, and JHQ shortly had more dramatic events to enquire about. As time passed and we became more confident we ignored their more asinine requests and only passed on what we thought important, which of course was our proper function.

Time was running out fast now, however, and we were well aware that all the peace initiatives had failed and that the Iraqis couldn't physically get out of Kuwait within the parameters of the UN Resolution even if they'd wanted to. At this stage I was still completely unaware of any plan which existed to oust the Iraqis from Kuwait, although I knew that some of my colleagues were a bit better informed than I. It didn't take too much imagination to work out that any operation would probably start with some sort of air attack, but that's about as much as I had thought about it. We all knew it was coming soon.

The night shift reported for work at 2130 hours on the night of 16 January, and we were instantly aware that something was going on. Nobody said anything, nor was there anything out of the ordinary happening, but we could feel that the atmosphere was quite different. There was something intangible about the place, an unspoken anticipation which set us all on edge. We went for "lunch" at midnight as usual, a meal taken outside the HQ in a lean-to shed in the back yard where the RAF cooks produced standard forces fare which had come as a welcome relief after the first few weeks existence on Wendy Burgers and little else. As we munched our sausages and chips, I was aware that there was a seemingly endless succession of aircraft taking off from the airport. I mentioned this to Richard Aubrey-Fletcher, who looked at me in a funny way and said that he thought that maybe "something was going on." At that point I knew that he knew, and that I was about to find out.

Sure enough, I was back at the Ops desk at 0150 in the morning when the Assistant Chief of Staff Ops (ACOS Ops) announced that US forces had just launched 100 cruise missiles at Iraq. We were briefed formally at 0200 that hostilities against Iraq had commenced. At long last the air war had started.

PART 3

Distant Thunder

CHAPTER IV

We were actually briefed just about the same time as the first raids were starting, although we learnt that US special forces had gone into action at 0120 hours, forty minutes beforehand, to neutralise some Iraqi radars and allow some of the Coalition aircraft to penetrate the Iraqi border undetected. Suddenly aware that it was all really happening, we turned to the television with a kind of awful fascination to confirm what we had just been told. CNN[24] was broadcasting live from Baghdad and were quick to pick up that something out of the ordinary was going on. What none of us realised at the time was that the first raids against Baghdad were being made by the F117A Stealth Fighter, which has the radar cross section "equivalent to that of an insect" and is therefore virtually invisible to normal air surveillance and warning radars. Consequently the Iraqis had no warning whatsoever of the air raids on their capital city and were reduced to reacting blindly after the event, resulting in those television images of anti aircraft fire spraying wildly into the night sky which we remember so well.

Back in Riyadh we were immediately plunged into a series of air raid and NBC warnings which had us struggling in and out of our cumbersome NBC suits and concentrated our minds somewhat. Nothing came our way, of course, but it did add to the excitement of the occasion. I think I was rather in awe of events at this stage, wondering how on earth we had come to this sorry state and yet rather pleased that I was there and had a very small part in it. My fascination grew as the statistics became available; 382 sorties[25] against 156 targets by Coalition air, with the RAF flying twenty-four Tornado GR1[26] sorties against five airfields with all aircraft returning safely despite, so we were told, a "brush" with MIG 29s[27] on the last raid. We heard that the Americans had destroyed the Presidential Palace in Baghdad, but elsewhere had lost an F18[28] from their aircraft carrier the USS Saratoga. The French apparently had four Jaguar[29] aircraft hit by small arms fire, though none were lost, on the second wave of attacks. There was absolutely no way we could confirm or refute any of this at the time, and of course strictly speaking it was nothing to do with the Land Cell, but it was heady stuff and we couldn't help becoming involved. When I left the Ops Room at 1100 the next morning there was a note on the board stating that RAF Tornados had neutralised three Iraqi airfields and had destroyed three MIGs. All that day bombing raids continued, as they were to do right up until the end of the war, and some 1400 sorties had been flown by the end of the morning of 17 January. Sadly, the RAF lost their first two Tornados, but we believed their crews to be alive although probably captured. Iraq's response was virtually nil, and there were already some reports of large scale defections and surrenders.

On the second night of the air war we had great excitement. At about 0300 we were notified of an Iraqi missile launch against Israel.[30] This in many ways was the nightmare scenario, for if Israel responded there was some speculation as to whether the Coalition would survive. Our Arab allies were unlikely to support an attack by their traditional enemy against one of their own kind, albeit one who was unpopular and ostracised. There was much scurrying to and fro plus frantic 'phone calls from London, and eventually we determined there had been eight missile launches in all: three landed in Tel Aviv, two in Haifa where one reportedly hit a ship, two dropped short in Iraq, and one was unaccounted for and never confirmed. During all the drama we had almost instantaneous television coverage showing in the Ops Room.

These missile attacks had two fairly dramatic results. In HQBFME we received reports which suggested evidence of nerve agent[31] attack had been identified, and we got decidedly twitchy. Our NBC officer in HQBFME was a comparatively junior Captain, but on his shoulders fell the decision on whether or not we should start taking our prophylactic medicine against nerve agent poisoning, called NAPS.[32] With time at a premium, allowing no time for referral to a higher authority, he very rightly decided that we should start taking our NAPS tablets straight away, and as we were the national HQ in theatre the decision was passed to all British units in the Gulf. At a stroke 43,000 men and women began to prepare themselves against the awful possibility of chemical attack. While this was all going on, US forces fired their Patriot anti aircraft system at an incoming missile and destroyed it at 13,000 feet over Dhahran, their main port of debarkation. It was later claimed to be a Styx missile, launched from a ship, which neatly tallied with an Iraqi gunboat being sunk by a US Navy aircraft at about 0500 hours.

SENDING MY LAUNDRY FORWARD

Meantime, Israel had scrambled an AWACS and seventy-six combat aircraft to strike back and, unbelievably we thought, had secured agreement to transit Syrian airspace to reach Iraq. The Coalition and Israel came to a speedy arrangement over deconfliction of airspace over Iraq, and a line was drawn down the chart in the Ops Room showing the demarcation. Thankfully wiser counsel prevailed and the attack was never launched, but for a short time we felt ourselves looking into the abyss. Saddam Hussein's strategem did not succeed, but it had been a close run thing.

In the middle of all this General de la Billière arrived in the Ops Room, having been woken as events unfolded, and was none too pleased at how he found it. Although we were all well versed individually in the workings of HQs, having practiced on countless peacetime exercises preparing for just this sort of event, the HQ was not yet operating as a cohesive unit. There was no procedure for briefing him, for example, nor was any individual nominated to do so. We had undoubtedly allowed ourselves to get carried away with the excitement of it all and had lost a firm grip on the situation. He had a few quiet words with the senior officer on duty and departed with a bit of a steely glint in his eye, having no doubt stated his future requirements and standards quite clearly. To his eternal credit, however, there were no histrionics or bad tempers, and he neither embarrassed nor humiliated those who had not, on this first occasion, been quite up to the mark.

All became quiet again about 0630, and there was little activity for the rest of that particular shift. Even at that point it was apparent to us all that Saddam Hussein's failure to goad

Israel into retaliation was a most significant event. Had Israel become involved then at least some of the Arab members of the Coalition may well have found it impossible to continue as part of it, and the very real spectre of the Coalition failing through lack of cohesion could have arisen. As it was, Israel was rewarded for her constraint by the immediate despatch of US Patriot batteries to protect her population centres from ballistic missile attack and the political situation stabilised for the time being at least.

During the next day the air war raged on unabated, and by the time we returned to the Ops Room the following night we were able to watch some of the film taken by our aircraft during their attacks, the most interesting of which never made it on to national television. Aircraft losses stood at seven after two days. All sorts of strange rumours were now circulating, including one which alleged that the Iraqis had a missile armed with multiple chemical warheads and a range of 5,000 kilometres which was going to be launched from Mauretania! The real excitement started about 0300, however, with reports of explosions and possible chemical agent attack at the FMA at Al Jubail. Both types of chemical agent detectors deployed there, the Chemical Agent Monitors (CAM) and Residual Vapour Detectors (RVD) gave positive responses, and for a while there was a bit of a flap as everybody masked up in their respirators and chemical recce patrols were deployed. I received a report on the secure telephone link that a propeller driven aircraft had been heard overflying the FMA just before the alarm, and we really believed that there had been a chemical attack, probably blister agent, a particularly nasty and debilitating concoction extensively used in the First World War and much "improved" since then. A flash signal was sent to London and Ministers were briefed, for this was indeed serious and had important political and military ramifications. In the end, though, it all rather fizzled out, for the NBC boys were unable to confirm the presence of any known chemical agent and there were no casualties, thank goodness. Perhaps some other relatively harmless chemical set off the alarms, but we never found out, nor did we ever identify the mystery aeroplane which had been heard. It was a false alarm, and the best that can be said of it was that it provided a useful exercise in NBC defence for the troops.

As we slowly wound down and started to think about the end of the shift we got the word that another four missiles had been launched against Israel. One landed forty miles south of Tel Aviv, a second somewhere west of Jerusalem, and the other two we knew not where. F15s flying CAP[33] moved in immediately to take out the launchers. The General's brief that morning[34] updated us on aircraft losses, and total Coalition losses now amounted to ten, with corresponding Iraqi losses standing at twelve, including six of their total of forty-one MIG 29s. Twenty-four hours later the Coalition aircraft casualties had risen to sixteen, and comprised: one F18 from the USS Saratoga, three RAF Tornados, one Italian Tornado, two Saudi Tornados (ran out of fuel), three F15s, one F16[35], one F4G Wild Weasel[36], two A6-Es[37], one OV-1[38], and a Kuwaiti A4[39]. This was quite a toll in only three days' fighting, and if it continued the Coalition's total losses might well reach the 170 aircraft and 150 pilots which US planners predicted. Most worrying for us was the loss of yet another RAF Tornado, this time shot down by a surface-to-air missile (SAM) over Tallil airfield so we believed, with the crew killed. All three RAF Tornados lost came from the same squadron based at Muharraq in Bahrein, and as there were only nine Tornado aircraft in total there at this point it represented a 33% loss. The press had already picked up the fact that RAF losses were disproportionately high and were debating the matter intensely. I can't say we were particularly surprised, for the Tornados were being used for low level attacks on Iraqi airfields using the JP233 runway cratering weapon, the use of which dictates flying straight and level down the enemy runway at about seventy-five feet above the ground for maximum effect. All the Iraqis had to do was fire their weapons straight up in the air and wait for the Tornados to fly into the barrage.

The fourth night of the air war, that of 20/21 January, was to be the most dramatic as far as we on the night shift were concerned. As we arrived in the Ops Room three SCUDs were fired at Dhahran, the main US port of disembarkation in Saudi, and there were a few tense moments until we heard that five Patriot missiles had been fired to intercept and the US forces claimed all incoming missiles destroyed. All went quiet again until we went for our "lunch" at midnight, taken as usual in the lean-to shack in the back yard of the HQ. Word came of yet another missile alert as we were savouring our sausage and chips, and then a cheerful clerk opened the back door and told us that this time it was Riyadh. Quickly we scrambled into our Noddy suits while our food went cold, and then we were treated to the sight of three or four Patriot missiles launched by the US battery up at the airport flying off into the clouds and detonating at least two incoming missiles. It was a bit like Guy Fawkes night for a moment, then we remembered that these SCUDs could possibly have chemical warheads so we quickly masked up.[40] At this point Richard Aubrey-Fletcher and I decided that our proper place was in the Ops Room so we ran down the street towards the main entrance. As we did so, another missile was intercepted and detonated directly over our heads with a quite thunderous roar and flash of red. It was rather like being caught in the middle of a severe thunderstorm, except the lightning flashes were bright pink, and it was most exciting and spectacular. I remember quite distinctly that the dust on the street "bounced" at the point of detonation. For a short while it seemed as if there were missiles flying everywhere and I think all of us were slightly in awe of the immensity of it all. We remained fully masked up for forty-five minutes or so while the chemical and biological warfare recce parties went out and did their stuff. Interestingly, the Americans did the chemical investigation but only we British seemed to have the biological expertise at that time.

It became clear later on that the missile expenditure that first night had been enormously extravagant, with thirty-five Patriot fired to intercept just six SCUDs launched at Riyadh. Command and control of the Patriot units was apparently the problem. There were three batteries round Riyadh at this stage in the proceedings, but they were not yet controlled centrally. The Patriot system was designed to launch two missiles at each incoming unfriendly missile to assure a kill. Each of the three batteries tracked six SCUDs and, as there was no centralised fire control system in place, each fired twelve missiles (one misfire) at all six SCUDs. The end result was a firework display which surpassed even the famed Glenlivet Firework Concert at Edinburgh Castle during the annual Festival, and which no doubt eventually presented the Saudi government with a bill far in excess of that justified by the actual threat.

Funnily enough, this first raid on Riyadh gave a major boost to the morale of those working in HQBFME. Until this point we had been collectively a little ashamed of our cushy lifestyle while the boys roughed it out in the desert. But now we had been the first to come under attack and, despite the lack of real danger, we could at least claim that we had been fired at in anger! I believe it went a little way to defuse some of the perfectly understandable resentment the front line troops felt and brought us all a little bit closer. For my part I lost no time in sending my Regiment back in Germany a signal notifying them of my claim to be the first member of the Royal Tank Regiment to come under fire in the current conflict, a message sent with my tongue firmly in my cheek and one treated, no doubt, with a certain amount of derision on arrival. We did feel, however, that we were now really at war and that the conflict was no longer just something we saw on our television screens.

A number of similar missile attacks occurred over the next few nights. On the night of 21/22 January we had a false alarm to start with, followed by the real thing at about 0330. Two SCUDs were fired at Riyadh, and six Patriot fired to take them out. A little surprisingly only one of the SCUDs was intercepted and the other left a five metre square crater out on the airport road. The booster part of this missile separated and fell in the road outside Air HQ! We began to realise that, good as Patriot undoubtedly was, it was not perfect and a number of the incoming missiles inevitably got through.[41] This was reinforced the very next night when another missile attack was launched from Iraq at Israel. Despite the attentions of the Patriot batteries which the US had supplied to Israel the missile hit a suburb of Tel Aviv and injured about seventy people. Nobody was killed by the missile strike, but apparently there were three deaths from heart attacks in the ensuing mayhem and excitement. Once again the Israelis did not retaliate, although rather ominously they said they retained the right to do so at a time and place of their own choosing.

The following night was much in the same vein. Having moved HQBFME to a new, more spacious office block over the past few days (and one just as unprotected as the former one), I had to nip back to the old place to collect a couple of things from my desk. As I drove back to the new building the air raid sirens started up again. All hell was let loose on the roads as Saudi drivers, ignoring all the road signs and traffic lights in their panic to get away before the missiles fell, drove at breakneck speed with horns blaring in a mad attempt to get home. I roared back to the new building, stuck on my gas mask, and ran into the HQ past the Queen's Own Highlander guard who were struggling into their kit having heard the bangs of Patriot being launched out at the airport. On getting to the Ops Room I was declared superfluous and sent to shelter in the basement. After about fifteen minutes we got the all clear and I drifted back upstairs. It appeared that two missiles had been fired at Riyadh, and there had

Me with locally sourced RTR baseball cap. British Army Training Unit Suffield (BATUS), Canada

Alistair Fyfe, OC D Sqn, on recce with SSgt Dryburgh

My tank at BATUS

C Squadron 4RTR, BATUS, August 1990

C Squadron 4RTR, my command, at BATUS in night time leaguer

My 2ic, Captain Patrick Kidd, briefs off the map at the front of his tank

'Bombing up': loading ammunition for the next day's firing

Sgt Barnwell's tank bogged on night march

Me at Lake Louise, Alberta, on R&R

Jolyon Jackson at Lake Louise

Early briefing at HQ British Forces Middle East
(HQBFME)

Major Richard Aubrey-Fletcher, Grenadier Guards, at work in
the Land Ops Cell, HQBFME

Riyadh taken from the top of HQ building

Sentry position on roof of HQ building

HQBFME first location. British Forces Post Office (BFPO) in prefabricated shed

HQBFME sentry at his post on the roof

Richard Aubrey-Fletcher (left)

Chris Manning, Army Air Corps (right)

Jonathan Campbell-James, Intelligence Corps (left)

Marriott Hotel, Riyadh. Our home for most of the war.
By the end I hated it.

Our accommodation when we moved temporarily
from the Marriott Hotel

Loading onto Hercules at Riyadh airport

HQBFME going up country after war ends

US tanker aircraft at Riyadh airport

"Highway of Death". Kuwait to Basra Highway 80

"Highway of Death". Kuwait to Basra Highway 80

Sunset over the desert: taken while driving back to Riyadh from HQ 1 Armd Division

The end: HQ 1 Armd Div, Iraq, after combat operations ceased

The end: final location of HQ 1 Armd Div, Iraq

The end: exhausted soldiers of the Queen's Own Highlanders
in a Hercules aircraft

been two impacts – ten nautical miles north and six nautical miles northeast of the city. Two SCUDs were also fired at Dhahran, and two flashes were seen in the sky near Bahrein by HMS London. One was also reputedly fired at Israel but further information was not forthcoming. I calculated that to date the Iraqis had fired thirty-one missiles and had killed one person; as a military weapon the SCUDs had proved to be pretty poor, but they had considerable political impact and an ever increasing amount of time and effort was being directed to counter this particular threat.

At the same time as these events the air war continued unabated. The RAF lost another two Tornados over the period, bringing total losses to five in combat and one to a malfunction. We all knew something was wrong somewhere, for the US were flying four or five times as many sorties but were losing barely twice the number of 'planes. The media had picked this up and the press was full of speculation as to the causes. The aircrew of the first Tornado to go down, Flight Lieutenants Peters and Nicol, were paraded on Iraqi television together with a number of US aircrew. Peters in particular looked pretty badly beaten up, and there was a great deal of anger in HQBFME when we saw the state of them on the news. Despite the immense air effort, however, there were some doubts as to its effect. We still lacked proper and comprehensive BDA[42] to confirm what we hoped had been achieved, although it seemed that the total number of sorties – approximately 10,000 by the morning of 23 January – *must* have been some impact on Iraq's military capabilities, especially as they seemed to be unable, or unwilling, to do anything about it.

SENDING MY LAUNDRY FORWARD

There was also some skirmishing on the Iraqi – Saudi border on the night of 22/23 January. The US 3rd Armoured Cavalry Regiment (3ACR) killed six-eight Iraqis and took six prisoners, whilst elsewhere the Saudis took twelve prisoners. On the same night, and on a slightly lighter note, the British medical unit 32 Field Hospital was nearly captured intact as it drove up country from Al Jubail in the middle of the night, missed the turning to join the remainder of the Division in the desert, and was only stopped just before driving right into Kuwait! What a PR disaster that would have been, although it was easily enough done. A little later in the campaign two officers from HQBFME, who will remain nameless, nearly did exactly the same. One, newly arrived in theatre, drove, while the other, after giving instructions on how to get to Divisional HQ, fell asleep in the passenger seat. It was only when the driver began to pass dug-in T62 tanks[43] with gun barrels pointing in the direction of their car's travel that he woke his companion. They had strayed into the area occupied by Egyptian troops and were only a few kilometres short of the border. Suddenly mindful of the interesting documents they were carrying, they hurriedly turned about and made good their escape.

Things began to settle down after the mayhem of the first few days into a gentler and slightly more recognisable pattern. We were rapidly becoming mystified by the lack of Iraqi reaction to the onslaught. Their navy was being destroyed piecemeal, their airfields, command control and communications centres, and political/military/economic assets were being slowly eroded away, and their one serious air sortie to date had been shot out of the sky by Saudi F15s.

On top of all this, the Iraqi army was being hammered in situ from the air, with one of their Republican Guard Force Divisions[44] being bombed every half hour by US B52s.[45] The only slightly ominous sign was the increasing number of Iraqi aircraft which were being allowed into Iran, some of which seemed to be afforded an Iranian fighter escort as they crossed the border. There were fears at this time that an Iraqi ELINT[46] Boeing 707 was operating against the Coalition from within Iranian airspace. The Iraqis had also begun to pump crude oil into the Gulf, presumably to set it on fire at a future date to deter an amphibious landing, or perhaps merely to create an environmental hullaballoo and another media weapon to use against the Coalition. But apart from these there was little other reaction of note and our intelligence briefings had a much more optimistic ring about them. There was even some speculation on whether Coalition ground forces would need to go into action at all given the predicted successes of the air campaign.

CHAPTER V

There was no let up in the air war as the end of January approached. The RAF Jaguars were in action during daylight hours, attacking targets such as ammunition dumps in Kuwait which they did on 25 January, returning without loss. The Tornados continued to fly deep into Iraq despite their losses: a typical night like 25/26 January saw them attacking three targets – six aircraft against the Al Mahawil SAM[47] depot, seven aircraft against the Tall Allahm ammunition storage site, and ten aircraft plus three ALARM aircraft[48] against the Al Diwathiyam communications site. All these aircraft returned safely, thank goodness. Other Coalition aircraft continued to attack Iraqi ground units, and we began to see the first evidence that the RGFC in particular were being hit hard as they tried to send forward some AFVs and artillery pieces to replace those damaged or destroyed. Over one twenty-four hour period Coalition air flew 112 F16 and twelve B52 sorties against the RGFC, with one Division in particular, the Hammurabi, getting most of the attention.

The SCUD raids continued but had lost some of their effect through familiarity and the fact that rarely was anyone hurt or anything damaged. An exception occurred on the night of 25/26 January, when two missiles were fired at

Riyadh. Four Patriot were launched to intercept, but there was still an extremely loud bang seemingly close outside HQBFME as at least one warhead got through. We were masked up for twenty minutes while investigations were carried out. Apparently some damage was done to a building further in towards the centre of the city, and perhaps one person had been killed and several injured. We now had developed a little routine for dealing with these attacks. On first alarm, non essential personnel went to the basement, which offered a modicum of cover, and stayed there until the all clear sounded. Of those left, usually two of us on the Land desk, one made all the necessary 'phone calls to inform JHQ, the Division, the FMA and so on what was happening. The other got into his NBC suit, and then roles were swapped. On average this took about four minutes and, as we knew by now that the normal time which elapsed between attack warning and the missile arriving was about eight minutes, we spent the remaining four minutes reading the newspapers, telling jokes, chatting, and watching the clock. It was always quite a relief when we heard the missile land and knew we were unharmed, but eventually we became quite blasé about it all. Even the local citizens became relaxed about air raids and were frequently seen scrambling on to the rooftops with video cameras to record the SCUDs' arrival.

I received my second anthrax and whooping cough jabs, plus one against against bubonic plague, which came as a bit of a surprise. As expected, these made all of us feel pretty ropey, although we did laugh when we heard that the senior medical officer responsible for all of this had taken the following day off because he felt unwell! Personally, I'd have dragged myself into work even if half dead to avoid the embarrassment. I was a bit surprised to learn that GOC 1 (UK) Division had told his command to stop taking NAPS, contrary to the HQBFME instructions. A bit risky, we thought, bearing in mind the opposition's extensive chemical arsenal, and we hoped he knew what he was doing. The Division was now well into the desert and involved in work up training while moving towards TAA[49] Keyes, in which they planned to be complete by 31 January and from which they would go into action if all the last minute diplomatic initiatives failed.

To our great delight we all became "SCUD aces" the next night when Riyadh was attacked for the fifth time. Eight missiles were fired in all by the Iraqis, with six going to Israel, one to Dhahran, and one at us. Damage in Riyadh was negligible. The exit of Iraqi aircraft to Iran was continuing and was a bit of a mystery. We all rather hoped that they were defecting, but there was always the possibility that the Iraqis were planning to mount an anti-shipping attack from inside Iranian airspace. We didn't discover until later that it was a desperate gamble by Saddam Hussein to try and preserve part of his air force, and that the aircraft were actually being interned and would not be returned to Iraq even after the war had ended. Around this time it also became clear that the Coalition had more or less achieved air supremacy and we were able to fly at will over Iraq. The destruction of eight Iraqi aircraft without loss to ourselves in three separate incidents showed that, to all intents and purposes, the Iraqi air force was now out of the equation as far as the rest of the war was concerned. The RAF brought out six of its venerable

Buccaneer aircraft, originally designed for low level anti-shipping strikes but now re-roled to mark targets for the Tornados to bomb from medium level using precision munitions – in other words laser guided bombs.[50]

But the Iraqi army was still a force to be reckoned with, and the night of 29/30 January saw the first significant moves on the ground for some time. It began with reports from the area occupied by the US Marine Corps, more or less directly south of Kuwait City, of enemy tanks crossing the border and concern that some of the Marine OPs[51] had been overrun. Then we got reports from two other Marine Corps OPs of Iraqi cross border incursions including one straight down the coast road towards the Saudi coastal town of Ras Al Khafji. The situation was extremely unclear for most of the night and we were unsuccessful in our attempts to get more detailed information. Eventually we heard that the Marines were claiming fifteen enemy tanks destroyed for the loss of two of their Light Armoured Vehicles (LAVs), one of which apparently had suffered a "K" kill – ie had blown up. Later, at about 0200, we heard of enemy tanks at the "tri border area" – ie where the borders of Saudi Arabia, Kuwait, and Iraq joined. Initial reports of thirteen tanks plus unspecified numbers of armoured personnel carriers (APCs) soon reduced to three tanks which a US SF OP engaged. US A-10s[52] were tasked to deal with these, but the Iraqi tanks hid in the village of Al Ruqi where there was the possibility of confusing them with nearby Egyptian armoured units, so they were let alone. By about 0400 it appeared that all the enemy were back north of the border with the possible exception of a few to the north of Khafji.

SENDING MY LAUNDRY FORWARD

When the intelligence boys briefed the next morning that the enemy action might well have been a two brigade operation we were flabbergasted. There was no evidence of any attempt to mount a coherent combined arms operation, nor had there been any sort of artillery preparation. If this had been a deliberately planned attack then we were tempted to deem the threat laughable. Whatever the truth was, at the end of the day Iraqi remnants remained in Ras Al Khafji, surrounding a US Marine Corps reconnaissance company, and themselves boxed in by the Saudi Arabian National Guard. The situation was *very* confused. Eventually the Saudis and Qataris went in to winkle the Iraqis out, and for a long time we knew nothing except a rather quaint report that friendly forces "had destroyed a tank and surrounded a house which they thought had Iraqis in it." Sadly one of the US AC 130s[53] which was supporting the operation stayed around too long after daybreak and was shot down, killing all the crew. Later the US Marine Corps admitted eight-ten KIA and about twenty WIA.[54]

Elsewhere the war progressed well, with some success recorded at sea against Iraqi patrol craft in the Gulf. Our Sea Skua missile[55] was not performing well, however, and on one sortie, from two launches, one was a "hang up" and the other dropped straight into the water. More ominously we heard reports of an Iraqi "chemical associated" artillery battalion being moved south to Basra. One or two interesting points arose at the morning brief following the Ras Al Khafji skirmish: one was that four Salvation Army officers were coming out into the theatre of operations, prompting General Sir Peter to comment that "I've got God under command now." The other item of much more interest to our sartorial elegance and general morale was that we would shortly be issued with our desert combat uniform, allowing us to at least dress for the part. We had looked enviously at our US allies in their "chocolate chip cookie" desert uniform for long enough and longed to be on a par.

★ ★ ★ ★ ★

As February arrived things became noticeably quieter overall. There were still missile attacks by the Iraqis on both Saudi and Israel, but we had by this time become really blasé about them and sometimes they were not even mentioned in the handover between shifts. There had been some amusing moments during the earlier raids: during one, Charlie Wiggin had scrambled down to the basement of our new living accommodation dressed only in boxer shorts and gas mask. During the raid he fell asleep, and at the all clear was left there as a joke by his fellows. The poor chap woke some hours later, frozen, disorientated, and still wearing his gas mask, swearing a terrible revenge on those who had left him. On another occasion, the same individual and Ian Rodley were out in a local restaurant when the sirens sounded. Assuming it was yet another false alarm they continued with their meal and laughed at the antics of the waiters, who had one gas mask between them and were taking turns at breathing through it. They quickly stopped laughing when things started going bang in the sky, and to their dismay found that their NBC kit was in the car and they couldn't get out because the waiters had locked the door! Being gassed in a burger restaurant because you had forgotten to take in your NBC kit is not a particularly glorious way to appear on the casualty list. Thankfully none of the raids were chemical.

After the "Battle" of Khafji things had settled down on the border as well. The final casualties for this skirmish were given as: Iraqis, eleven tanks, nine APCs, thirty-five KIA, thirty-five WIA, and 411 PW. Coalition casualties were given as three tanks, one multi launch rocket system (MLRS), two ambulances, eighteen KIA, thirty-five WIA, four MIA, and nine PW.[56] Typically, both the Iraqis and Saudis claimed a great victory. Our assessment was that the Iraqis had definitely been repulsed, but not with great ease. The Saudis had enjoyed an immense amount of US assistance, mainly in the form of air support, and yet it seemed to have taken them rather a long time. Khafji apart, there were all sorts of rumours circulating almost on a daily basis about large Iraqi vehicle movements north of the border but they never came to anything. Even if they had been true, JSTARS[57] allowed them to be spotted as they formed up and bombed before they had a chance to move. For the Coalition it was truly the "transparent battlefield" and the enemy were always at a severe disadvantage.

Not surprisingly, with so little going on that affected us, life at HQBFME became a bit dull. On the night shift in particular there was very little to do. We all made the most of the spare time to write home, and I must have written to nearly everybody I could think of whose address I knew. I was also pleasantly surprised by the letters I received from friends of whom I had not heard for many years. I even got a couple of 'phone calls from civilian friends while I sat at the Ops desk – how on earth they got the number I never found out. Compared to the boys in the desert and elsewhere in Saudi, we were very lucky to have access to telephones. There was no barrier to using the civilian telephone system to 'phone home, and indeed from time to time my friends in the desert would ring on the military system and ask me to contact their wives and tell them that all was well. "Freephone Saudi Arabia" was another of the major perks of working in HQBFME and everyone took advantage of it. I shudder to think what the final bill must have been, for some called their wives and sweethearts every night for forty minutes or more. Rumours were constantly circulating that the day of reckoning was approaching and that all calls had been traced and bills would be issued. On one famous occasion a spoof bill for many thousands of pounds was issued on official paper to one of the most profligate culprits, sending him into deep depression until he was let off the hook. In the end, however, we all got away with it. On reflection I suppose it was freeloading at best and plain old theft at worst, but at the time we rationalised it being a legitimate extra for defending somebody else's country.

We also had installed a computer system, the so-called Desert Interim Computer System (DICS), which we could use for a variety of other, non operational, uses. I spent hours perfecting the technique of printing the blue airmail aerogrammes with which we had been supplied on the printer of this new system. Others played computer games, the most popular of which was strip poker, in which a variety of young lovelies would peel off their clothes on the screen if you were any good at cards. I wasn't, but there were some experts by the end of the war, and there was always a cluster round the screen when anyone was doing particularly well at the game. Kind souls in Britain sent us out a variety of presents, most of which quite rightly went up country to the FMA and Division, but we were well catered for in terms of books, cassette tapes, and even cakes. Antoinette sent me a poppy seed cake in the shape of a heart for Valentine's Day and I suffered a certain amount of leg pulling on account of it, but nobody was reluctant to eat it when they were offered some!

None of us were particularly enamoured with what little we saw of Saudi social life. We had expected a male orientated society, but I don't think any of us were quite ready for the true extent of it. The women were very much in the background, and we seldom spoke to any. Funnily enough, when we bumped into them without any Saudi men around, in the lift of the Marriott for example, they were very quick to open the conversation, but as soon as a male Saudi entered they returned to silence. I used to watch the men socialising at night in the hotel, a ritual which seemed to consist entirely of having coffee with the male members of their family, and think how sterile their social life was. This, of course, was an entirely ethnocentric judgement, but I just couldn't see how they enjoyed themselves. A social life without alcohol is easy and no barrier to fun, but the absence of women is quite another thing altogether. Rumour had it that the women's custom of dressing in black from head to foot and wearing a veil gave them complete anonymity and allowed them to take part in all sorts of indiscretions, but I doubt it very much. We referred to them as "Guinness bottles" or MBOs – Mobile Black Objects. I felt very sorry for the Saudi women and, correspondingly, a degree of antipathy towards the Saudi male. As for the country as a whole, it felt to me as if a society of simple peasant people had suddenly been granted riches beyond their wildest dreams in the space of a generation and were struggling to come to terms with it, which of course is more or less exactly what had happened.

Morale got a fillip on 5 February with the announcement that the Saudi government was going to give us all a medal, so all 43,000 of us were going to have something to hang on our chests afterwards. We all hoped that the British government would also authorise a campaign medal, as in fact it did, and wondered whether the Kuwaiti government would follow the Saudi lead. I think we had visions of returning with chestfuls of medals clanking as we marched in the victory parade down the Mall. In fact, the award of medals was to become one of the more emotive issues of the war, together with the payment of allowances, the issue of desert combats, and the provision of hire cars, of which more later. We all thought that we were entitled to them having been in theatre and fired at by the baddies, but we became quite irritated to hear that, for example, those working in JHQ High Wycombe considered themselves worthy recipients. Where did one draw the line? In the end it was sorted out amicably, but there were all sorts of anomalies. A celebrated example was those attending a polo course in Cyprus, which was technically in SCUD range, receiving the Gulf Medal despite having absolutely nothing whatsoever to do with the campaign. I was pleased to hear that some Commanding Officers had banned those who "won" their medals in this way from ever wearing them.

SENDING MY LAUNDRY FORWARD

★ ★ ★ ★ ★

A couple of nights later the Americans dropped two 15,000 lb airburst bombs on the Iraqis, and we were later to see video footage of them being launched from the open cargo bays of Hercules transport aircraft. For the first time I heard doubts on the morality of our actions being raised. It seemed an awful lot of death and destruction to impose on people who were essentially defenceless against air attack by this stage, and some of us didn't like it very much. We hoped that the US forces weren't just using the war as a convenient testing ground for their weapon systems. It was interesting to see that, even in a war which most of us felt was justified (even although we were generally cynical as to the *real* reason we were there), a strong sense of "fair play" remained. This feeling was to emerge again later in the war when the Iraqis were caught from the air on the Kuwait to Basra highway, the infamous "Highway of Death".

About this time I met Mark Urban, the BBC Newsnight journalist, in Riyadh. He had been a TA officer in 4RTR back in the early 1980s and I knew him quite well, so we had lunch at the Marriott. By this time I was totally au fait with the Coalition ground attack plan, and naturally Mark sounded me out on what I thought would happen. I said nothing, of course, but by starting from first principles he already had an extremely accurate view of how the ground plan might unfold. For a start, he knew that 1 (UK) Division was not where we said it was but much further west. He also had assessed that the terrain from which he correctly guessed the Division would start lent itself perfectly to a wide armoured left hook into northern Kuwait, thereby cutting off and isolating the bulk of Iraqi troops there. In fact he got most of it right, which shows that he hadn't forgotten much of his military training. I'm just surprised that the Iraqis hadn't worked it out too. After our short meeting he went off up country and occasionally we heard all sorts of unfounded rumours of him bluffing his way into various units and headquarters, but I didn't see him again during the campaign.

Over the next few days the picture remained roughly the same. The Iraqis were getting hammered from the air and seemed completely incapable of doing anything about it. We began to wonder if soon there would be anything left to bomb. It seemed incredible that they were just going to sit there and take it, and that Saddam Hussein did not intend to start political moves to bring the whole thing to an end. Work became seriously dull, at least for the night shift, and a lot of us began to wonder exactly when we might hope to get home again. Not for the first time a feeling of being unable to control events, of one's destiny being decided by the whims of others, affected many of us. Morale wasn't exactly poor, but we were getting decidedly fed up. I suppose it was rather akin to being in gaol with no indication of the date of final release.

On 10 February the Foreign Secretary, Douglas Hurd, came round the HQ on a visit. I shook his hand and remember thinking how ill he looked. He was terribly nice, and I attempted to brief him off the large scale map on the current situation but not terribly successfully. It wasn't helped when he said something along the lines of "So this is where the Division is" and pointed at a spot on the map about

500 kilometres off its actual location. To be fair, I reckoned that he had enough on his plate at that point and the precise location of our chaps was probably the least of his worries. At least he came round to say hello and broke up the general tedium.

We did, however, now know the date of G Day, the day the ground offensive was due to start. John Cantwell came down to Riyadh from Divisional HQ looking for any information we could give him on Iraqi dispositions in the path of the Division's projected advance. Despite the Coalition's array of sophisticated surveillance and target acquisition systems and its ability to fly at will across Iraq, the troops in the front line had very little information on the enemy at the tactical level. The intelligence system was simply swamped by the vast amount of information being gathered from all sources and very little properly sifted intelligence filtered down to those at the sharp end. In particular, the Division wanted photographs of the Iraqi positions in its path and I think we were successful in getting a few Tornado sorties' worth for them. The Americans didn't seem to be capable of getting this sort of low level information, although their strategic and operational level stuff was remarkably good. John described his task in the forthcoming operation and quite frankly I didn't think we'd see him again. He made the most of his stay in the Marriott and had his first bath, followed by a few more in quick succession, for a month. It was apparent that the boys in the desert now wanted to get on with it and get it over and done with, which was hardly surprising.

On the 14th the news was dominated by the deaths of

approximately 500 Iraqi civilians in a bunker in Baghdad which was destroyed by two bombs from an F 117. This was very sad, and all sorts of recriminations were flying round, including the allegation that Saddam Hussein had deliberately put civilians in the bunker for propaganda purposes. The US authorities were adamant that it was a communications centre and therefore a legitimate target. There was a thought that the incident might lead to a swing of public opinion (and most importantly American public opinion) against the war and that the land campaign might be brought forward as a result. No such swing occurred, but the media played on the disaster for many days afterwards. It was a terrible event and we in the HQ felt awful about it. For all the trumpeting there had been about the new generation of precision weapons and the reduction in collateral damage, in the end innocent civilians had still been killed and injured. We hadn't really progressed very far over the last fifty years or so.

Despite the furore, the US XVIII Airborne Corps began deep cross border helicopter recces the next day, the first significant conventional ground force operations into Iraqi territory. Against this background of deepening involvement we were somewhat surprised to learn of the peace proposal broadcast on Baghdad radio which contained the first mention by the Iraqis of a possible withdrawal from Kuwait. This raised everybody's hopes and was hotly debated. A couple of days later the conditions of the offer were softened by the Iraqi Ambassador to the USA, and the conditions became "issues" which could be discussed at a later date. However, someone had done a little appreciation in the

SENDING MY LAUNDRY FORWARD

meantime of the logistics of an Iraqi withdrawal and it became clear that they had no hope of getting out in time, so we had returned to pessimism. It really didn't look like there was any chance of resolving it without some ground forces action.

A number of operations took place over this period, including some cross border incursions by helicopter and ground troops. In the XVIII Corps operations already referred to the helicopters which went deep into Iraq saw little, while the ambushes they put in place across the border reported no action. They did, however, attack an enemy EW[58] site with Apache[59] helicopters although we never got to know the results. In the US VII Corps area (1 (UK) Armoured Division was by this time under command this organisation) there were some skirmishes and one Iraqi tank and another vehicle were claimed destroyed. In addition, however, their Apaches had managed to knock out two US vehicles – a Bradley IFV and M113 APC – with US casualties of two dead and six wounded. We reckoned that this was, by our calculations, the eleventh time the Americans had fired upon friendly troops, although it was the most tragic incident to date. There was also the suspicion that the RAF might have killed some Iraqi civilians during a bombing raid on bridges on 14 February, and the media were not slow to pick this up. Later we saw video footage from the attacking aircraft which confirmed our worst fears: at least a couple of bombs had failed to be guided properly to the target and had hit the village beyond. How very sad.

PART 4

Lightning Strikes

CHAPTER VI

By the time we got into work for our next shift it was G Day. Saddam Hussein hadn't bothered to respond to the Coalition ultimatum, and so at 0100 hours Greenwich Mean Time on 24 February it all started to happen – the biggest land operation since the Normandy landings in 1944, so we were told. As is well recorded elsewhere, the Coalition attack was phased, that is it had different elements attacking at different times to catch the Iraqis unawares and deceive them as to where the main effort lay. At H Hour, 0400 hours local time, the American XVIII Corps and the French 6 Armoured Division, on the Coalition's western flank, were first off the mark into Iraq and made remarkably quick progress. In the eastern part of the theatre, the US Marines attacked north into Kuwait and towards Kuwait City and almost immediately had the strange and unforeseen experience of being hampered by surrendering Iraqis as soon as they breached the border berm. By about six hours into the operation they were some thirty kilometres into Kuwait and it appeared that there was nothing to stop them.

Even at this early stage in proceedings we began to wonder if it might not all be over much faster than was originally thought. We were really rather busy for the whole shift, briefing JHQ on developments as far as we could –

communications with the Division were poor – and looking to see if we could bring the schedule forward if the enemy were routed. The COS, Colonel Ian Talbot, was buzzing around like a bluebottle on amphetamines and quickly became known as the "rogue Patriot" for his resemblance to a missile which had lost its guidance. The pace was frenetic but eventually settled down as we became used to working in the climate of constant change and imperfect knowledge. As the end of the first day approached the Division was all set to go, just waiting for the US 1st Infantry Division (Mechanised) – the Big Red One, as they liked to be called, or 1ID for short – to secure the breach in the border berm and minefields.

The General's morning brief took on a whole new significance now that ground operations had started, for we in the Land Cell could take a much fuller part. The night shift was responsible for the 0800 brief, and I often marked up the main briefing map at around 0630 as part of the preparation. While the land battle was in full swing General Sir Peter frequently came into the briefing room from his nearby bunk in dressing gown and slippers, hair tousled and mug of tea in hand, to get an early informal update on what had happened overnight. Such was the uncertainty and difficulty in getting accurate information from the desert that I fear he sometimes left these early morning sessions not much the wiser, for I recall that I had often to reply "I don't know" to his questions. I'm sure he realised the difficulties we faced and was always understanding of our lack of knowledge. We usually were a little better informed by the proper brief at 0800, but we never really got any information on the fortunes of our Arab allies apart from BBC and CNN news reports.

These formal briefs always followed the same format. The RAF watchkeepers spoke first with a weather forecast[60] for the next twenty-four hours followed by a review of air operations over the last twenty-four hours. We were on next, with me briefing on the flow of Coalition land operations in general then Richard Aubrey-Fletcher on the progress of 1 (UK) Armoured Division in detail. The Navy came next, and then a host of others on supply, medical, PWs, etc. It usually lasted about an hour and was videotaped throughout. I must say that once again I was struck by the similarity of the whole proceedings to a Staff College exercise at Camberley, and it was sometimes hard not to regard the assembled audience as the Directing Staff (DS) who had come to assess and mark one's performance! I rather enjoyed these briefings in the end, for I quickly realised that, although I knew very little of what was happening across the theatre, most of the audience knew considerably less and therefore my confidence grew exponentially over the few days of the land campaign.

The ground campaign made dramatic advances over the next twenty-four hours or so, and when I returned to work in the late evening of 24 February the picture was quite different. On the extreme left flank of the Coalition forces the French 6th Armoured Division[61] had moved very quickly indeed on to its first objective, and by first light on the 25th was well on the way to its second one, Objective White. Next to them, the US 101st Air Assault Division had placed two brigades about 120 kilometres into Iraq and had secured Forward Operating Base (FOB) Cobra, to which it had begun to transfer all the necessary equipment to sustain operations deeper into Iraq. Next to them in turn, the US

24th Infantry Division (24 ID) and 3rd Armoured Cavalry Regiment (3ACR) left their line of departure (LD) at first light on the 25th and went full tilt for their objectives, deep inside Iraq, which they reached in six hours. In the VII (US) Corps area, the Coalition's main point of effort, the troops started a day later in accordance with the plan for a staggered start. The 2nd Armoured Cavalry Regiment (2ACR), 1st Armoured Division (1AD), and 3rd Armoured Division (3AD) all shot off at dawn to take on the Republican Guard, while 1ID pressed on with their breaching operation with 1 (UK) Division tucked up close behind and keen to move quickly. To their right, the 3rd and 4th Egyptian Divisions, plus the enigmatic Task Force Khalid, prepared to breach the border obstacle. Yet further east, the US Marine Divisions which had had such success in the opening hours of the land offensive continued to take enormous amounts of prisoners – up to 13,000 in their area alone. Finally, the Joint Force Command East (JFCE) forces of Saudi Arabia and Kuwait broke through the obstacle belt nearest to the sea and advanced at a slightly slower pace into Kuwait, supported from the waters of the Gulf by the guns of the USS Missouri.

It was breathtaking in its scale and yet the enemy failed to respond. Perhaps, rather like us, they were almost mesmerised by the drama as it unfolded, and were somehow rendered unable to do much about it, or perhaps it was the Coalition's mastery of the skies which kept the bulk of Iraqi forces stationary and concealed. There were minor movements of various Republican Guard units reported but these amounted to very little compared to the immense movement of Coalition forces. Even at this early stage we became critical of our own success, and much ado was made on the morning of the 25th that the British Division had not yet moved through the breach made by the Americans. This theme was to resurface on a number of later occasions and I had to agree that compared to our US allies we sometimes appeared pedestrian and lacklustre in the speed of our Division's manoeuvre, but in this case it was solely because 1ID took rather longer than anticipated to move its third brigade through the breach. I took a number of agitated 'phone calls from JHQ from those who rather irritatedly asked "what was wrong with our Division", and did my best to explain.

When I left work at the end of our shift, around midday, the Division was on thirty minutes notice to move (NTM) and its leading elements were already into Iraq, albeit just a little and stationary. Op Trebor, the HQBFME draft plan to move elements of our HQ into the British Embassy in Kuwait as soon as was feasible, was being dusted off. We suddenly realised that we might well be in Kuwait long before we had imagined. I must admit it was hard at this point to fully understand exactly what was going on in the desert. Our communications were sometimes temperamental, we were living in a luxurious hotel and driving to work like everybody else, and were in no real danger. For us the whole affair was always in danger of degenerating into a gigantic board game because we were so distant from the action.

When I returned to work twelve hours later I found matters had continued to progress apace. Coalition movement continued across the front, but most noticeably in the 101 Air Assault Div area, where US troops had cut

Highway 8 and were on the Euphrates by 0700 hours on the 26th. Our Division was now making steady but sure progress against minimal Iraqi opposition, but there was now a definite feeling abroad that we were being seen as slow and plodding when compared with the Americans, who seemed to be shooting ahead everywhere. Such was the optimism and lack of concern for any enemy air threat that our air defence gunners were being used to guard the 600 odd Iraqi PWs which the Division had collected to date. British casualties were incredibly low, with one Royal Corps of Transport driver killed and five other wounded men. US casualties were light too, and far below many of the estimates made before hostilities.

We briefed General Sir Peter twice that morning (26th), once at 0600 – with him in characteristic pyjamas, dressing gown, and slippers – and once again at 0745. I did the big picture as usual, attempting to describe the ebb and flow of operations across an ever widening front, and Richard Aubrey-Fletcher covered 1 (UK) Div's movements in detail. It seemed to go quite well. The boys for Kuwait were chosen, that is those who were to set up HQBFME (Forward) in Kuwait, and to a mixture of disappointment and relief I wasn't one of them. When this operation had been first mooted I had been warned off as a likely participant, and no sooner had I heard than I was being measured up for a flak jacket which I was assured I would need! The plan had been that we chosen ones were to land at the British Embassy building in Kuwait City on the second helicopter, the first having carried in the special forces who were to have secured the landing site. We were also told that the landing site was likely to be "hot", ie still in the middle of a small arms fight, and I had all sorts of visions of either being machine gunned on arrival or shot down by some over zealous Coalition soldier as we flew in. So I wasn't *too* disappointed not to be going! As it happened, the Iraqis had fled by the time our chaps went in and there was, thankfully, no bloodshed.

When we left at the end of our shift, subsequent operations were being planned, a phrase that encompasses all the planning for what was likely to happen next. The general feeling was that the war couldn't possibly last very much longer given the scale of the Iraqi defeat to date and that something had to give rather sooner than later. We had heard that Saddam Hussein had at last ordered his troops to quit Kuwait, but we didn't know where they could run to now that the Americans had cut Highway 8, the most obvious route back across the Euphrates and on to Baghdad.

Once again, when we returned to work an all too short twelve hours later the map had changed dramatically. The Americans, having secured the Coalition's western flank with 6 (Fr) Div and 101 (US) Div, started to turn to the east to take on the heavy divisions of the Iraqi army stationed on the Kuwait/Iraq border. We had come to expect US formations to be remarkably quick off the mark and once again they did not disappoint. They moved with breathtaking speed. In contrast, our Division was still puffing away as it rather methodically defeated the Iraqis in its path. To be fair, we had started a day later than many, and we were unfortunate to be bogged down with so many PWs who hampered manoeuvre considerably. Nevertheless there is little doubt that we looked very ordinary when compared with the Americans and not a few people commented accordingly.

By the morning of the 27th all Iraqi troops were in the process of attempting to get out of Kuwait, except for the Republican Guard which seemed to be holding firm. All the routes out of Kuwait, however, were cut by Coalition air, and the end result was a huge pile up of vehicles. The Iraqis were jammed on four lane highways with nowhere to go and the skies were full of every aircraft the Coalition could get into the air trying to destroy them. The end result was illustrated dramatically by the television pictures of the Kuwait to Basra highway – "the Highway of Death" – which soon found their way on to our screens. We heard through our liaison officers that some of the US pilots were sickened by the one sided destruction which was going on along those jammed routes, and not for the first time the morality of such a one sided contest was called into question.

At the morning brief General Sir Peter reckoned it would be over in about twenty-four – ninety-six hours, which filled us all with relief. The HQ "stepped up", that is to say we sent a small party forward to Kuwait to set up HQBFME (Land) (Forward), as Op Trebor came to fruition. It was done so secretly that nobody really knew what was going on, and there were a few misunderstandings and antics not unlike a Brian Rix farce before it proved easier to let everybody know what was happening so we could do it properly. It was becoming clear that, with the war almost certainly won, the next major task was going to be getting everyone and everything out of theatre and back whence they had come as soon as practically possible. Planning actually started in earnest well before the ground war was over, and the first teams flew out from Britain to the Gulf on 27 February. At the end of this particular shift I recall that we were all a bit tired and bad tempered, and I think the handover to the incoming relief was probably an ill humoured affair.

I also had an opportunity that day to talk to my CO in Germany, Martin Speller, about what the future might have in store for me. The Regiment had this idea in its collective head that I should go and work next in the RAC's personnel branch, PB17, in Stanmore in Middlesex. This post, I was assured, was "a good thing to do for my career." The bloke actually doing the job at the time told me it was a post of real power, and used the fact that he had sent me to the Gulf as an illustration of his omnipotence! I had absolutely no desire whatsoever to become a personnel manager at that stage in my army career, and was wise enough by that time to realise that whether the move was or wasn't good for my career was peripheral: the post needed to be filled and I was available, nothing more. Eventually I managed to wriggle my way out of it, thank goodness, and have never had cause to regret it.

Of more pressing interest, however, was the news that my Regiment, 4RTR, to which I would return at the end of the Gulf crisis, had been chosen to do a six month tour in Cyprus as part of the UN forces there, commencing in June. The Regiment had in fact completed just such a tour in 1989 and under normal circumstances would not have been expected to return so soon, but such were the exigencies of the Gulf that we were asked to go again. Now, I had had my fill of Cyprus on the first tour, and while two weeks on that desolate, cheerless island would have been bearable, the thought of another six months made me pale. Worse still, it would be an unaccompanied tour with wives only there for holidays, and it would have been most unfair to abandon Antoinette again so soon after the first desertion. Luckily the CO was sympathetic to such views, and with much relief on my part he agreed that I should be Officer Commanding Rear Party, basically looking after the families and vehicles in Germany while the Regiment was in Cyprus.

With that not inconsiderable weight off my mind, I returned to work the next day to find that, as we were told breezily, the war was nearly over. The US swing from the western flank across the desert to cut off the enemy had made astonishing progress, and the Iraqi forces in the Kuwait Theatre of Operations (KTO, we always called it, thinking ourselves cool) were completely cut off. We were really just awaiting details of a much rumoured ceasefire deal to be announced by George Bush, and all operations were on hold. At 0430 hours local I was informed by the ACOS Ops that a cessation of hostilities would be imposed at 0500Z[62], 0800 hours local. I only remember being rather nonplussed that the war appeared to be about to end so undramatically – no driving to Baghdad, no sensational capitulation by Saddam Hussein, and no real sense of victory. It was rather in danger of being a bit of a damp squib. Kuwait City had been relieved and was constantly on the television, to which we turned once again as the only real time information available. We were most grateful that the BBC had replaced CNN as our staple diet, for the difference in quality and depth of reporting was all too obvious, and we got a much more balanced view of events as they unfolded.

It was quite apparent that the Iraqis had now completely collapsed and were streaming north back towards Baghdad, being harried by Coalition air as they went. It had got to the point, I thought at the time, where to continue to attack the vast majority of the Iraqi forces was no longer morally justifiable, a view which was shared to a greater or lesser degree by many of my colleagues. And yet Saddam Hussein had not yet capitulated.

At 0500 local the US President announced the "suspension of Coalition offensive combat operations" in three hours time. The conditions were as follows:

1. Iraq was to immediately release all PWs and third country nationals.
2. All Kuwaiti detainees were to be released.
3. The locations of all land and sea mines were to be notified.
4. All UNSCRs, including acceptance in principle of the compensation issue, were to be accepted.
5. Within forty-eight hours designated Iraqi commanders were to meet their Coalition counterparts to arrange the military aspects of the cessation.
6. The UNSC was to meet to formulate peace arrangements.

No sooner had we heard the announcement than we were rather astonished to hear from the Division that VII (US) Corps had ordered them to resume offensive operations again. The guys in Divisional HQ were really bushed by this point, having been on the go since before the breaching operation. Their speech was slurred on the telephone and they had difficulty summoning enthusiasm even for the end of hostilities. Anyway, they told us that they had been given fresh orders to continue attacking to the east and destroy as much enemy armour as possible before the ceasefire came into effect. Now, we really *did* think this was excessive by this stage in the war, and many in the Riyadh HQ gave voice to their disquiet. Nevertheless, it went on for another three hours and then it stopped. We all just hoped that it would stay stopped.

PART 5

The Clouds Pass

CHAPTER VII

When we returned once more to work in HQBFME, in the late evening of 28 February, it appeared that the war was indeed over, even although there had been no formal ceasefire or acceptance of the Bush conditions. We only now began to get a true feel for the scale of the Iraqi defeat, and it was enormous. We were led to understand that to date 3,008 tanks, 1,856 APCs, and 2,140 artillery pieces had been accounted for, mainly abandoned by routed Iraqi troops but many destroyed. By all accounts thirty-seven Iraqi divisions had been defeated, and there seemed to be no cohesive Iraqi defence left whatsoever. The Americans were planning to blow up most of the abandoned Iraqi equipment starting the next day, except of course the stuff which was to be kept for "exploitation"[63] or for display purposes, the latter a euphemism for war booty. JHQ sent out a demand for captured equipment which made us all laugh to the core – it included 100 T72s, 100 BMPs, and so on, which was just cloud cuckoo land. I think in the end the Brits ended up with only three T72s, and even they were "stolen" from the Americans if I recall correctly.

By all accounts the former battlefields were awash with weaponry, and every unit which was represented in the KTO was determined to get a tank at least, plus a slack handful of other assorted lorries, small arms, and other trophies, back home to Germany or Britain to display on the Regimental square or in the Regimental museum. Fairly strict guidelines were promulgated almost immediately, but it wasn't too long after the end of hostilities that an Army Air Corps officer flew back from the Gulf into Brize Norton and presented HM Customs and Excise with two AK47 assault rifles which he wanted to import. That piece of crass stupidity effectively queered the pitch for everyone else. I was quite keen that 4RTR should have something or other to commemorate all the officers and men who had served with other units in the Gulf, and I went to some lengths to secure a couple of rifles when I got back to Germany. I even got as far as getting display cases made for them, but I lost track of them when I was next posted. To this day I don't know what became of them.

All efforts were very quickly directed towards getting out of the region as soon as was humanly possible. We had all had more than enough of the Middle East in general and Saudi Arabia in particular, and we were by now desperate to get home. Nobody lost their sense of humour, however, and I remember chuckling when the first humorous sketches and leaflets began to circulate. One example, no doubt dreamt up by some wag in the wee small hours of the midnight shift, said:

REHABILITATION CENTRE
RIYADH
SAUDI ARABIA

Dear ...   Date ...

You are hereby warned of the forthcoming return of ... to the United Kingdom in the month of ...

He will be dehydrated, demoralised, and somewhat darker in colour than when you last saw him. Do not be alarmed, remember the crude environment which has been his miserable lot for the past… months. You are warned, therefore, to take note of the following points whilst he is with you, for at least the first two weeks.

DO'S

(a) When he arrives at the airport, send someone to meet him. In the interest of public decency this must be undertaken by a male member of the household.
(b) Lock up all females between the ages of nine and ninety and fill the fridge with his favourite beer. Warn all non-whites living locally not to make any sudden movement in his presence.

DONT'S

Do not mention any of the following in his presence: Saudi Arabia, Riyadh, petrol, lovely sunshine, guards, deserts, haircuts, sand and holidays by the sea.

Do not feed him: lamb, beans, chicken, tinned peas, pepsi cola or curry.

Do not be alarmed if he reads old newspapers, screams with delight when it rains or, when given such rarities as pork or bacon, shouts *"Taman Mangiera"* (lovely grub), or greets everybody with *"Haef Haalik"* (how are you), or upon hearing a car horn, yells "Get knotted bloody ragheads, what else did Allah send you for Ramadan?" (like Christmas), snarls at children who come near him *"Imshee mafeesh buckshees"* (Go away, I don't give donations), or walks around the house in nothing but a towel, humming "We gotta get out of this place".

Until you feel he is his old self again, do not let him out on his own. When shopping, if he bargains with local shopkeepers, explain that he means well, just comfort him and lead him from the shop.

If, when finding no cup of tea (MUST NOT BE MADE WITH TEA BAGS) brought to him in the morning, and he should shout *"Sadik"* or *"Jibli"* (friend), the best plan is to dress up the smallest member of the family (male) in a dirty towel, smear boot polish all over him, and send him running and shouting "Coming *Sadik*" (Coming friend).

He will probably be frightened seeing the following: buses, trains, trees, pubs and women, be patient and just explain quietly what they are. A must for you is to buy an English/Arabic phrase-book, with this you should be able to teach him English in a very short time.

> Bear in mind that beneath that rugged tan beats a very strong heart of gold. Treasure this, it is the only thing of value he has left. Treat him kindly, and with tolerance and an occasional pint from the fridge you will be able to rehabilitate that which is now a hollow shell of the happy man you once knew.
>
> Signed ...

I think the anonymous author of this bittersweet little leaflet summed up as well as anybody how we all felt at the time; not being able to better it, I sent it to Antoinette as part of one of my letters home, hoping she would find it as amusing as we did.

Optimism roamed unfettered as we began to calculate just how soon we might be able to leave Saudi Arabia. Some said as soon as within six weeks, assuming the first of 7 Armoured Brigade could move in about ten days time, working on the age old army rule of "first in, first out." There was a sense of fin-de-siecle in the air, and it seemed that all we had to do was exchange PWs quickly, extract all our stuff, and we were off. Brilliant. We couldn't wait.

There was another side, of course, a darker and less happy one. The Division reported that it was finding living on the battlefield a very harrowing experience. They found themselves amongst long columns of burned out enemy vehicles, full of Iraqi dead, and the Iraqi prisoners they had taken were stuck out in the middle of the desert with little shelter. The realisation had also begun to dawn that the ratio of reported casualties did not paint the picture of a hard fought campaign. The Coalition had suffered "only" 200 or so dead, whereas figures of up to 100,000 were being quoted for the Iraqis.[64] Not one of our tanks had been hit, and nor did we believe had any of the Americans'.[65] I had an interesting conversation with one of the army press briefers, a man for whom hitherto I had little time, on the morality of continuing to attack a defeated enemy. I always remembered a veteran of the Falklands War, who had taught me at Staff College, describing how he had ordered his men to stop firing on retreating Argentinians after one of the battles around Port Stanley because, as he had put it, it was no longer morally sustainable. I had been mightily impressed. Ten years later the same dilemma was taxing a number of people, and this briefer was of the opinion that that the last twenty-four hours of the war had been quite unnecessary. I agreed. It had been rather like one of the old colonial wars, I felt, machine guns against the Matebele armed with assegais. The conflict had been a bit too one sided for my peace of mind.

Within twenty-four hours of the cessation of hostilities I had another of my all too rare days off. When we had first arrived in Riyadh there had been far too much to do to contemplate such a luxury, and we had worked all day every day. Within a month or so, however, it became clear that we were going to become very stale and fed up very quickly if we continued in this vein, so every so often we got a day off. The problem was that there wasn't that much for us to do outside working. Generally speaking nobody else was off at the same time, so there was no question of going off in company to play sport, explore, go shopping, or whatever. Riyadh wasn't exactly conducive to R&R[66], being a bit of a wasteland of motorways on concrete stilts and unfriendly high rise office blocks in the American idiom – a bit like central Birmingham, minus women and bars, and with the heating turned full on. I tended, therefore, to stay in the Marriott, catching up on my sleep, writing interminable letters, and reading the many books sent out by friends, family, and well wishers. There was an outdoor swimming pool, and the weather was generally good enough to sit out and do a little sunbathing. The pool was always swarming with RAF personnel, who I have to say produced some of the scruffiest looking servicemen in uniform I have ever seen. I was constantly amazed that their officers never did anything about it. Perhaps they didn't care, but the RAF's reputation took a bit of a beating on account of their slackness.

The hotel itself was depressing. It wasn't that it was uncomfortable, because it was as good as any hotel of that type I've stayed in, but it had no soul. There was nowhere to go outside one's room, and on venturing out regardless there was only ever a continuous stream of Saudi and Kuwaiti men drinking coffee in all male family groups. The corridors and foyer were full of noisy and chattering Kuwaiti refugee children at all hours of the day and night, for they didn't have anywhere to go either until they could get back to their country. Worst of all was the television. I still have bad dreams about Saudi television, with its hopelessly amateur Saudi programmes and its staple diet of overwhelmingly mediocre, and heavily censored, American imported programmes. These were interrupted several times a day for prayer time – nothing wrong with that, I hear you saying, and neither there was except that, for example, the film would be kept running during prayer and therefore you always rejoined it having lost about five minutes of the action! I never really realised just how superior the BBC actually was in every aspect of television programming and production until I stayed in Riyadh. Saudi TV would undoubtedly have driven a lot of us to drink had there been any available.

After a day off I returned to work during the normal day shift, a welcome relief after seven weeks of constant night shift. There now was very little for me personally to do, as we were still waiting for the ceasefire to be finally agreed. "All out in forty-two days" became the great cry, but for the moment we sat around waiting for something to happen. I moved back to my equipment oriented job which I had done before the war properly broke out. There wasn't any requirement for me on the Ops desk anymore (there weren't really any ops to speak of now) and a host of equipment related matters now came to hand. Not least of these was the need to find out how both our and their equipment had actually worked for real, and so a slack handful of data collection groups moved into theatre to glean the relevant information. Rather uncharitably, perhaps, I saw them as overly keen to get in on the act and play desert warriors before it was all over. This was one of the great paradoxes: the Gulf was full of people whose only thought was to get out as quickly as was humanly possible, while elsewhere there were scores of people who were quite desperate to get involved. I remember a Johnny-Come-Lately in my Regiment telling me how lucky I had been to have been out there all through he war, and me thinking how daft he was. I would have swapped with him any time.

The other matter which began to take a certain amount

of our attention at this point was the planned Bahrein equipment exhibition. Some cynical opportunist in the British government had decided that we should capitalise on both our rapid victory and the presence of much of our armaments industry's products in the region by participating in the post war arms sales jamboree in Bahrein. This I found most distasteful. It was rather as if the dead Iraqis strewn across the desert and the fact that "combat proven" could now be stamped all across the literature was proof of the quality of our products. I have always thought the morality of the arms industry to be pretty dubious, and to try and sell our stuff on the back of a one sided war was tacky and insensitive. Surely this was truly the "unacceptable face of capitalism", and such rampant and base commercialism so soon after the event made a mockery of those on both sides who had risked their lives. Apart from some outline administrative planning I had nothing to do with it and was glad that it was so.

Such concerns took only a small part of our days, however, and life became tedious once more as we waited to hear when we might go home. In Iraq there was some thought that the country might be on the threshhold of revolution and the overthrow of Saddam Hussein. We got a number of reports of shelling in Basra and once again rumours of the possible use of chemical weapons. We were sad for the Iraqi people, for the last possible thing they could have wanted at this point was yet more violence. Recovery of Iraqi weapons and equipment from the battlefields continued all the time, and I was desperately trying to persuade all who would listen that 4RTR needed an Iraqi

T55 as a gate guardian, for we certainly had enough of our soldiers in the theatre to justify it. Alas, all my efforts were in vain and my suggestions fell on deaf ears.

One very important task HQBFME had, however, was to help compile the Post Operations Report or POR[67]. Like most other large organisations, the British army tries hard to review what has been done in training or in operations to identify strengths and weaknesses and improve performance the next time. This is reasonable enough and will not surprise anybody. However, the difference between the Services and most other large institutions is that we are not called upon to ply our trade for real as often as, say, the Fire Brigade or British Airways. There is habitually a large gap, maybe as much as twenty or thirty years, between us carrying out our post mortem on one war and applying the lessons learned in the next. Consequently, we are open to the criticism that we usually enter the next war well prepared for the last, and often with disastrous results. A classic example is the First World War, which the British army entered having rectified the deficiencies in musketry and fieldcraft which had been exposed in the Boer War, but with scant preparation for the industrial nature of the new European warfare. Nevertheless, it would be a foolish organisation which did not try to learn from past successes and mistakes, and we set to. A team of about twenty or so assorted arms and service representatives left Riyadh in the very early hours of 6 March to visit the British units in the field and quiz those who had been closest involved in the fighting before memories dulled.

We flew from Riyadh to Al Jubail in an RAF Hercules, which was pleasant enough, but it was raining when we arrived at our interim stop. The aircraft then developed a fault, something to do with the rudder not operating properly (I always remember thinking that the fault must have happened in the air, because you don't use the rudder on the ground very much, but I never asked), and we could well have been stuck. If it had been peacetime we undoubtedly would have been, for the RAF is notoriously slow and inefficient at fixing its passenger transport aircraft. We would have been looking at a twenty-four hour sojourn in the basic facilities at Al Jubail airstrip at least. However, one of the joys of being on operations, in the Gulf at least, was that air transport was able to throw off the shackles of peacetime restrictions and operate *properly*. If you wanted to go somewhere, and there was a 'plane going with some room left on it, you got on, simple as that. What a relief it was from the tiresome and grossly inefficient beaureacracy of RAF peacetime transport operations!

Anyway, there was an RNZAF Hercules on the strip and it was available for tasking, so we transferred to that lock, stock, and barrel for onward passage to Kuwait International after a two hour pause. I think the NZ crew might have been a little hacked off, for I seem to remember that they were about to go off duty after a normal shift, but they did their best to hide it. They had an extremely laconic Sergeant Loadmaster who addressed everyone in our party as "mate", regardless of rank, which confirmed what most of us already thought about him and his countrymen. He was quite amusing, however, apologising for the lack of in-flight movie in his pre-flight briefing which he must have given dozens of times since arriving in theatre. In the end they delivered us safely and without incident to Kuwait International, despite the restricted visibility from the burning oil wells[68], and we were most grateful.

The airport had been pretty badly knocked about by Coalition aircraft during the war and presented a desolate spectacle as we deplaned. There was a burned out airliner close to where we arrived and the runways were strewn with shrapnel. Every pane of glass in the large terminal buildings seemed to have been broken, and it looked as if the place had been thoroughly looted. We didn't have much time to explore, though, for shortly we heard the clatter of helicopters and two or three RAF Puma[69] helicopters hove into view and taxied up to collect us. The HQBFME party was to split into smaller parties and visit various units scattered across northern Kuwait. I and several others were bound for the Divisional HQ, located some dozen miles or so beyond the outskirts of Kuwait City, on the way north to the Iraqi border and Basra.

As we flew across the city I noticed that there were quite a few abandoned Iraqi tanks and other vehicles by the sides of the roads, both in the centre of the town and in the residential suburbs. Nothing had really prepared me, however, for the scene just outside the city on the main highway north. We flew at about 200 feet over what had become known as "Death's Acre" or the "Highway of Death" – the few kilometres of the motorway where our aircraft had trapped the fleeing Iraqis and destroyed everything from the air. Although I had seen television pictures of the carnage, the reality was if anything worse, and it was far from a pleasant sight. All lanes of the motorway were blocked by burnt out and destroyed vehicles, noses pointing north, and the sides of the road and far out into the desert on both sides was littered with the detritus of a defeated army in headlong flight. It was obvious that the Iraqis had commandeered anything that moved in their panic to escape, for amongst the tanks and trucks were large numbers of civilian cars, vans, and buses, similarly blackened by fire. Worse still, in many ways, was the evidence that all these derelict vehicles had been thoroughly looted, for each wreck was surrounded by a little pitiful pile of possessions which lay where the scavengers had discarded them. More than anything it was reminiscent of a large refuse dump, and to view it was hardly an uplifting experience. There was certainly no sense of triumph or victory as we flew over.

HQ 1 (UK) Armoured Division was in a plantation on the coast just north of Kuwait City, comfortable enough as far as living in the desert goes. The HQ consisted of the usual main Ops tent and so on, plus a ragtag collection of tents, trucks and assorted military and civilian vehicles parked in amongst the scruffy palm trees. I knew quite a number of people in the HQ by this time, including of course Duncan MacMillan from my own Regiment to whom I had often spoken on the 'phone during the war. They all seemed to be in fine fettle, if a little weary, and pleased that it was all over as far as we could tell. I spent up to midnight working in the main complex with Matthew Perkins, one of the staff officers, sorting out various details of who would be sent from the Division to the Bahrein equipment exhibition. After that I turned in for the night, sleeping in the 9x9 tent which was "owned" by Matthew and Tom Camp – a tight squeeze and not helped by the fact that Matthew had a complete arsenal of captured Iraqi weaponry under his camp bed! I woke up freezing in the middle of the night but my two companions seemed oblivious to the cold. I took this as a sure sign that my time as a pampered staff officer in the Marriott Hotel had made me soft – I had had no problems sleeping out in the cold of the Canadian prairies only six months before.

We got up at 0630 the next day, had a wash and shave in the local ablutions (outside, and cold water only), then went for breakfast. A very passable officers' mess had been established in the plantation owner's house, despite the fact that the Iraqis had done their best to smash the place up as they left. Working in the mess was LCpl Puddefoot, 4RTR, whom I knew well from Regimental days, and we had time for a chat about his experiences. After breakfast we went back to the main complex to put the finishing touches to the administration order for the equipment exhibition, then my work was done. I had time to read part of a book before lunch, when Duncan MacMillan drove me down in a civilian Range Rover to Kuwait City International Airport.

The number and variety of civilian cars with the HQ had surprised me, and once again I was reminded of another major emotive issue of the war. The Saudi government had been most generous in facilitating the hire of extra vehicles for the Coalition forces, and full advantage had been taken of the opportunity to add four wheel drive vehicles to our fleet for the duration of the conflict.[70] The allocation of such vehicles to individuals was a *very* sensitive topic, and apparently there was all sorts of unseemly squabbling amongst fairly senior officers over who got exactly what. The phenomenon was not confined to the Division itself, and the FMA and HQBFME saw similar petty jealousies. At Riyadh I overheard a Colonel instructing a Major to replace his perfectly adequate car with something more appropriate to his rank as he had seen officers junior to him driving better cars! I remember taking great delight in parading my borrowed Range Rover in front of more senior officers and claiming it was mine, for it never failed to get a reaction. It was all a bit pathetic really, and there was really no excuse: greed was the only motivating factor. The Gulf brought out the worst, as well as the best, in some people.

In any case, Duncan got me safely to the airport where I bade him farewell. We would next meet back in the Regiment in Germany. I found my way to the derelict office that extemporised as a check in desk where an extremely cheerful RAF corporal sat with his feet up and allocated passengers to flights. This wasn't too difficult for him, for there was a strictly limited number of destinations and if there was a flight going you got on it! Next to his desk was a tea chest full of Iraqi weapons, and he invited me to deposit any liberated firearms in my possession in it. I had none, and was slightly puzzled why this was deemed necessary, but later found out that a few of the Iraqi weapons had been booby trapped[71] and would have been a considerable hazard in flight.

The same friendly NZ crew were the ones flying me again, together with a company of Queen's Own Highlanders who had just come out of the desert and a few other odd individuals. There was also an extraordinarily pretty blonde American girl, serving with one of their Reserve units I think, on the 'plane. She had the lantern jawed, lanky, raw good looks reminiscent of those early photographs of the first settlers, and I guessed she probably came from Nebraska or somewhere equally remote. I wasn't quite sure what she was doing on the flight, nor was I sitting close enough to ask her over the rattle and vibration of the Hercules' fuselage, but about halfway to Al Jubail she disappeared upstairs into the crew cabin. About five minutes later the aircraft began to make some slightly peculiar manoeuvres, and I guessed that the pilot wasn't flying the aircraft any more. Sure enough, the blonde was the pilot's girlfriend and he was taking the opportunity provided by a routine flight to give his loved one some flying lessons! I wouldn't imagine for one minute that such practices were allowed even in the RNZAF, but nobody complained – we were all too tired anyway – and no-one in authority was ever the wiser. It made for an interesting interlude on a rather dull journey, and I was sorry when she left the 'plane at Al Jubail.

The remainder of the flight back to Riyadh was unremarkable. My old friend Jonathan Campbell-James was on the same flight and had arranged for an Embassy driver to pick him up at the airport. He very kindly offered me a lift home, which I accepted, and we diverted via his house for a couple of real beers before his driver deposited me back at the Marriott. This was to be my last trip up country, and the next time I saw the airport was to be on the way out of Saudi Arabia. The boys in the desert still had a little more time in which to kick their heels before they too headed for home.

CHAPTER VIII

Back at HQBFME the air reeked of end of term. Most of the POR team was still in the desert, but I had come back earlier than most to liaise, coordinate, and generally act as a link man for the equipment exhibition. There was still a certain amount to be done assisting in the recovery of the more attractive items of captured Iraqi equipment, most of which was being centralised near the FMA for eventual extraction back to UK. The SAS had its pick of the small arms and took a deal of the ammunition, for it trained on all types of weapons in case the need arose. We were also still, believe it or not, finalising the procurement of some of the Urgent Operational Requirements which hadn't quite made it in time for the war. An example was smoke marker rounds for our artillery; in the flat and featureless desert it's sometimes quite hard to spot, say, a well camouflaged enemy, and then usually even harder to point them out to everybody else. Smoke marker rounds enabled the Forward Observation Officers (FOOs)[72] to put a round of brightly coloured smoke in the general area and then give directions from that point. The problem was, after the Royal Artillery had asked for them, we couldn't find anybody who made them for love nor money. Eventually we discovered that the South Africans did, but as relations with the RSA were still decidedly frosty we didn't hold out much hope of that particular source bearing much fruit. But get them we did, all 5,000 of them, although I can't be sure where they came from. Sadly they were too late, but I dare say they're still in some ammo depot somewhere waiting for the next time.

It became clear that it wasn't just the smoke rounds that hadn't been necessary. Vast amounts of kit had been sent out to Saudi Arabia and never used, either because nobody knew where it was or because it couldn't be found. The main depot in theatre, 62 Ordnance Company, had expanded to cover many acres and there were literally thousands of containers and boxes there. Many of these were never even opened, let alone logged and distributed. Some front line units had become so frustrated by the normal supply system, which had quickly become overwhelmed by the scale of the task, that they resorted to sending their own men back to the depot to find the bits and pieces they so desperately needed. This further exacerbated the problem, for now there were additional bodies rooting through the unopened boxes looking for what they wanted. If any lesson was going to come out of the Gulf War, it had to be the requirement for a comprehensive stock monitoring procedure with some sort of asset tracking system to enable us to keep tabs on what had been sent and where it was stored. It isn't all that difficult, really, and civilian firms had such systems years ago, albeit usually working in less trying circumstances.

We did have a little bit of fun on the social side at this time, for all the permanent expatriate Brits in Riyadh did their level best to entertain as many of us as possible. For our part, we were free to move around Riyadh again and, more importantly, had some time off to do so. On one memorable occasion a few of us were invited down to the Diplomatic Quarter, to the residence of one of the British military representatives, for a cocktail party. Also at this party was a smattering of nurses from 205 Field Hospital, a TA organisation which drew most of its recruits from the Glasgow area. This organisation had been mobilised and sent to the Gulf in January, and at least one of the flights carrying its personnel had arrived at King Khalid International in Riyadh in the middle of a SCUD raid. This was indeed an unfortunate baptism of fire; it's bad enough arriving in a strange country in the middle of the night, but to be attacked and frightened and have to scramble into your NBC kit the minute you hit the tarmac is not an experience I would wish on anyone. It didn't seem to have caused the nurses at the party much harm, though, and they were in fine mood. We spent a very pleasant evening in their company, were careful with our alcohol intake, thanked our hosts and left. Our erstwhile companions were not so abstemious and several took full advantage of the drink they had not had since arrival in Saudi. An unfortunate and embarrassing episode then ensued on their departure; while shaking hands with her hostess for the evening, one of the departing nurses dropped two tins of beer which she had concealed under the cardigan carefully draped over her arm. We were highly embarrassed at this violation of our hosts' hospitality, but they never batted an eyelid. The girl responsible fled into the night after mumbled apologies. Perhaps we can put such shocking behaviour down to Post Traumatic Stress …

On 8 March it was decided to thin out the HQ, which

had expanded out of all recognition since the early days. Most of us were now spending our time just hanging around or spinning out our few tasks to take as much time as possible. Communication within the HQ was particularly bad at this point and it was difficult to find out what was happening or what the plans for the future were. However, we finally heard that individuals would not be told directly that they had become surplus to requirements and could therefore go home, but that if one's name did not appear on the list of personnel required to man the smaller HQ one could safely assume that this was the case! What an extraordinary way to run a HQ! I still find it astonishing that fairly senior officers, brought up in an army where much trumpeting takes place about leadership and man management, could allow this to happen. I hope those responsible for this particularly offhand and insensitive way of reducing numbers in what had been a hard working and dedicated HQ feel suitably ashamed.

I have to admit, though, despite the manner in which the information was disseminated, I was more than delighted when my name did not appear on the list. Why I should be let go early I did not question, only assuming that someone had taken pity on my short-lived attempt at married bliss to date. It only remained for me to check with my boss that I wasn't required further as far as he was concerned and I could start moving. I was greatly elated, as were all those in the first batch. I had always assumed that I would arrive back in Germany some time after the others who had gone into the desert, and had told Antoinette so, and now found that I would be first instead.

On 10 March I got final confirmation that my services were no longer required and started to make preparations to leave. The procedure was actually quite easy; the transport and movement gurus were in the same building and I simply had to find the first flight with space on it and book myself as a passenger. That done, all I had to do was wait, in my case for only four days.

I still had some work to do, however. I was spending a lot of time coordinating the ever increasing number of scientifically orientated visits we were receiving. Everyone was scrambling for data from the battlefield and, while we were never in danger of being overwhelmed, we preferred to have some sort of control over who was in theatre at what time. I also volunteered for one last nightshift to let Richard Aubrey-Fletcher, who was still on at nights after over eight weeks, have a break. I didn't mind in the slightest, especially now I could see an end to it all. As it happened, I only had one 'phone call in a five hour period after midnight, so I was sure that it really was time to go. The next day, after a late start, passed in odd 'phone calls and weeding the files which had sprung from nothing during our short time in Saudi. I also handed in my trusty NBC kit and posted my temperate combat kit back to Germany, thereby ensuring that I'd have no option but to swank back in my desert kit. I reckoned that was the very least I was entitled to after a three month enforced sojourn in the Middle East.

On 11 March my name actually appeared on the flight manifest for the coming Friday, which was outstanding news. Bitter experience has taught generations of servicemen not to expect anything to happen until it actually happens, but this was definitely a step in the right direction. I worked out that I could be back in Germany in time for breakfast on the day, and called Antoinette with the good news. That night in the Marriott we opened one of my colleagues' specially hoarded bottles of contraband in celebration, which was very generous of him as he had a few weeks to go himself before he was going home. Any alcohol consumed by this stage was referred to as "pre-treatment", a promise of greater things to come back in civilisation and a humorous reference to the NAPS tablets we had taken. It was an in joke to the BFME boys and another manifestation of the little exclusive club that had formed in adversity.

The next day was yet another long drawn out affair for me, except that it was broken up by General Sir Peter speaking to us all in the Conference Room at 1700 hours. He spoke very well indeed, pointing out the importance of everybody's efforts and stressing that we at the blunt end, as he rather nicely put it, had had just as important a role to play as those who found themselves in the front line. He was due to leave the Middle East in about two weeks time, no doubt, we thought, to take up the retirement he had delayed in order to become involved in the Gulf. He spoke to the whole HQ on another occasion, the exact date of which I cannot recall but close to this time, which was also well received. I well remember that he mentioned somewhere in this latter address that he had never done anything, or been posted anywhere, against his will in his army career. I suspect more than one or two of us made note of that and applied it in our own subsequent careers.

Finally, after what seemed like an age of waiting, my last

day in the Middle East arrived. I have to be honest and say I felt not one iota of sadness or nostalgia at the thought of leaving. It just couldn't have arrived quickly enough as far as I was concerned. I said my goodbyes in the HQ without too much fuss. Farewells in the Services are never very emotional events, because they are a normal part of everyday life and therefore expected. With a posting system that moves people on average every two years one can't afford the luxury of heart searching wrenches at every move. They are normal, and the chances are that you'll bump into the same people again in some other part of the world. So I just shook hands with everyone and left.

Typically, the flight left at 0220 hours local – the middle of the night again! Thus my little adventure ended as it had begun, at possibly the most psychologically inappropriate time imaginable for the journey. I used to wonder who actually chose such timings and whether they were aware of the effect the timing had on the passengers. I was also pretty sceptical about the flight leaving on time, for the one the night before had been five hours late. We were to leave from the same nightmare terminal I had arrived at some three months beforehand, with the same piercing lights and deep, forbidding shadows, with the same squaddies lurching sleepily to the makeshift lavatories in their singlets and flip flops, and with above all the same feeling of unreality. It was still an awful place and I sympathised with those who had spent the war there.

Despite my scepticism there was in fact no major problem. The flight was only forty minutes late, and it was a civvy one – British Airways doing their bit to take the boys home. The thing that brought home most forcibly to me that the war was indeed over was the weapons clearance procedure before we boarded; during the conflict we had become used to having weapons with magazines fitted about our persons, and we had merely ensured that they were not loaded, ie not cocked with a round up the spout, before getting on a 'plane. Now as we prepared to leave the theatre for the last time we had once more to go through the old peacetime routine. We lined up and cocked our empty weapons for inspection by the RAF loadmaster, looking for all the world like a bunch of cadets coming in off a school CCF[73] camp. That really brought me back to reality with a bump.

The atmosphere on the flight was understandably jolly, and we were to a man delighted to be going home. For the first time in my experience on a military flight we were handed a tin of beer and a half bottle of wine each, which added to the festive air. Obviously some wise man had worked out that the dangers of drunken mayhem on board flights out of Saudi were infinitesimal compared to the dangers of soldiers denied any alcohol over many months hitting the town centres of Europe and over-indulging. Accordingly, a pre-emptive strike had been authorised, so to speak. It was probably a very sensible move, for it took the edge off many ambitions to drink the nearest bar dry on return to civilisation. The immediate practical result, however, was to send everybody on the flight to sleep within about forty-five minutes of takeoff, and most remained that way until touchdown in Germany at RAF Wildenrath.

I had told Antoinette not to come to meet me, for it was

a long way from Osnabruck and there was no guarantee that my flight would be on time. I could only watch slightly enviously, therefore, as many of my fellow passengers were reunited with wives, families, and loved ones. Most importantly, though, the CO's staff car driver was there to meet me and take me home. I loaded all my gear into the boot of the car as quickly as I could and we were off. It was a long two and a half hour drive, and I felt decidedly odd in my sand coloured desert combat uniform as we sped past the damp green fields of the German farmland. But soon I was ringing the bell on my own front door, and Antoinette was opening it. Despite having had her photograph by my bedside since I left I had forgotten how pretty she was. It was great to be home.

PART 6

Aftermath

CHAPTER IX

I went on leave almost immediately, as we had all been promised whilst out in the Gulf. Just before departing there was a curry lunch in the Officers' Mess for the Gulf returners, all of whom had come home safely, thank goodness, in the space of a few days. I think that was the point where the war quite clearly came to an end for me, for it was so normal it appeared that nothing had happened in the interim period at all. Then we went on holiday, a combination of gentle tourism and visiting people we hadn't seen for a while. We very quickly christened it "The Victory Tour" – with tongue very firmly in cheek – for that's what it felt like some of the time. I think many people still remembered the vivid images which had been brought to them by television, and it sometimes took a great deal of effort to persuade friends and relatives that it hadn't really been all that dangerous, least ways not in Riyadh. Some were very wary of mentioning the war at all, and any reference to it was usually prefaced with the phrase "but I suppose you won't really want to talk about it much". In fact, I didn't mind talking about it in the least little bit and told everyone so, for some of it had been quite fascinating.

The most peaceful and restful part of my leave was spent in Switzerland, walking in the mountains. Antoinette's parents had a small home there for some years, being skiers, but we used it on this occasion as a base for gentle treks up above the valleys. After the noise, fumes, and concrete of Riyadh it was truly idyllic, and the best antidote imaginable. After five days and nights there I was quite refreshed and ready for the rigours of doing the rounds of family and friends in Britain, which I thoroughly enjoyed. In all I had five weeks' leave to savour, and at the end of it returned to Germany ready for anything.

It was, in fact, quite strange to be back to normal peacetime soldiering and all its niceties. For the first time I seemed to be aware of the trivial nature of much we did, and sometimes struggled to get excited about matters which obviously agitated others but to me seemed relatively unimportant. My days were quickly filled by a plethora of matters, ranging from training, discipline, and financial matters down to the more mundane reports and returns which are the bête noire of all desk bound Regimental officers. At least I couldn't complain of lack of variety.

Although none of us really thought overmuch about the last few months in the Middle East, I was left with three very strong and abiding impressions from my time there. First of all, the Iraqis had been much poorer soldiers, and therefore a much less dangerous enemy, than we had been led to believe. It is, of course, one of the cardinal sins of soldiering to underestimate your enemy, but I would suggest that it is almost as bad to overestimate him. While I am prepared to accept that until we knew better we were quite right to regard the Iraqi forces as equivalent to our own, we should have surely been more honest with ourselves and the rest of the world as time progressed. With the vast array of sophisticated intelligence and surveillance equipment at its disposal, the Coalition *must* have realised fairly early on that it was not up against a first class enemy. I refuse to believe that those directing the war did not know this, and still wonder what political imperative kept this information from the rest of us. Perhaps it was withheld to maintain the integrity of the Coalition itself, or more probably to keep the support of the public, and particularly the American public, without whose backing the alliance would surely have collapsed. Whatever the reason, the truth was that the Iraqi forces were never anything more than a third world army, dressed up in first world equipment perhaps, who had about as much chance of defeating the Coalition as the Dervishes had of trouncing the British at Omdurman.

Secondly, it was quite clear that the British Division had been slow and ponderous in operations and had never quite risen to the occasion. Too many years training to defeat the Warsaw Pact in northern Germany in a series of set piece battles seemed to have drained it of any dash and initiative. True, there had been a series of frustrating delays at the breach which had made for a slowish start, but such obstacles were soon overcome and should have allowed us to take full part in the breakneck dash into Iraq. Instead, while the Americans threw caution to the winds when they began to realise the extent of their victory, we were plodding our steady way through a series of half-heartedly held Iraqi defensive positions and complaining of being held up by hordes of prisoners when the enemy started surrendering in droves. I don't think there was much wrong with our soldiers, who did everything that was asked and more, nor was our equipment responsible for our fairly lacklustre performance. But I wonder if we really can breed the sort of commanders we need for this sort of high speed, intuitive, seat of the pants type of warfare. Fear of being seen to make a mistake has been a flaw in many of our senior commanders through history, and perhaps the overriding desire to have everything "properly teed up", to use Montgomery's phrase, prevented the Division and its Brigades being bold and decisive in its actions.

Finally, I had been most impressed by the competence of our American allies, who were the cornerstone of the Coalition and whose victory it really was. They had proved to be both thoroughly meticulous and professional in their planning, and then had prosecuted their plan with boldness and imagination. They appeared to have none of that air of enthusiastic amateurism which plagues we British, and were considerably the better for it. Yet, when presented with tactical and operational opportunities demanding instant decision and action, they had the self confidence and breadth of vision to seize the moment. Whether they had to prosecute the war quite so determinedly right to the bitter end is open to debate, but there could be no doubting their determination and tenacity. Man for man, I have little doubt that the British soldier is a little superior to his American counterpart, and below Brigade level we can probably give them a run for their money, but at Division and above we just can't compete. In the Gulf they were motivated, superbly equipped, and well led, and as long as they enjoyed the support of the American public probably had no equal. They won the war, and everybody else just tagged along.

Back in Germany life slowly returned to normal. 4RTR began to get back the parts which had been taken from its tanks when the crisis first erupted, and the long slow haul to get fifty-seven tanks fit again began. Eventually it was completed, but it took another year or so, and other forces outside our control had been at work in the meantime. The British government announced its "Options For Change" strategy for the armed forces, which was a Defence Review by any other name, and 4RTR's name did not appear on the new Order of Battle. The reduction in tension in Europe in the aftermath of the Cold War made much of our army in Germany redundant, and large amounts of our hardware were no longer required. In the end, the Regiment slaved over its obsolete Chieftain tanks to get them fit only to take them to Hohne Ranges[74] one more time, fire them during the last gunnery camp, and then hand them over to be scrapped. It was very sad, and an enormous effort for nothing.

It wasn't just the equipment which was obsolete; large scale troop reductions were also required and the army set forth on a round of voluntary and compulsory redundancies with some reluctance. Within twelve months of our return from the Gulf two thirds of the dozen or so of our Regimental officers who had gone to war had left the army. Most of them were forced to go, victims of their Short Service Commissions[75]; there was no room for them to extend their Commissions, as was the norm in days gone by, in the new slimline organisation. Those who had Regular Commissions were relatively safe in their careers. Funnily enough, most of those who had volunteered to go to war were Short Service Officers, and therefore those who were forced to retire were the very ones who had all the combat experience. We ended up with an officer corps experienced in orderly officer duties, barrack administration, and not a lot else. It was a crass decision, and I can think of no competent large scale commercial organisation which would have approached a similar problem by sacking its most successful and experienced salesmen. At a stroke the Royal Tank Regiment lost most of the operational experience in tank warfare amongst its officers.

I had expected that there would be a bit of jealousy or antagonism between those who had gone and the rest, many of whom had tried repeatedly to get a posting out to Saudi and had failed. My fears were groundless, however, and there was only a steady stream of fairly good humoured banter. The dozen odd of us who had gone presented one of the signed prints of the Terence Cuneo oil painting, which had been commissioned by 1 (UK) Armoured Division on its return, to the Officers' Mess. Rather cheekily, we had a plaque placed on it with the legend "Presented By The Officers Who Went To The Gulf To Those Who Did Not", which raised the odd wry smile but not much else. After a few weeks most of the decent war stories had been told, and talk of the war quietly died away.

For my part it had been an interesting three months, and in retrospect I'm glad that I was part of it, especially as we all came home. To be honest, however, I never truly felt that I got to grips with it properly. Sure enough, I did a little bit of useful work on the equipment enhancement programme, and I manned the Ops desk faithfully at night with my companions whilst the war was on. I even got fired at, after a fashion, and scurried for cover clutching my NBC kit on numerous occasions. But there is really nothing I can say that I personally achieved from beginning to end, and to that extent it was most unsatisfactory. My most lasting and vivid memory of the whole episode is an overwhelming feeling of not being in control and of being disposable at someone else's whim. If I had to choose one personal lesson from the experience it would be to beware of people with "good ideas".

I have often asked myself if it was all worth it, and the answer I invariably come up with is no. Rather naively, I suppose, and in common with most of my colleagues, I thought we went to the Middle East to aid a tiny defenceless state against a notorious bully and see justice done. But it became apparent early on in the proceedings that the international community would not have been half so outraged had Kuwait's main export been potatoes. As I'm sure must be blindingly obvious to almost everybody else, what the Coalition was actually engaged in was a fairly cynical exercise in political and economic self interest, with a bit of international justice added on for good measure. To safeguard Kuwait's oil supplies to the West we were prepared to fight on behalf of, and restore to power, a regime every bit as corrupt and loathsome as that of its immediate northern neighbour. I can't get any personal satisfaction out of that.

Operation Desert Storm may well have been second only to the Normandy landings in terms of scale of military effort, but it cannot compare when we look at long term results. After all the effort, and fears, and loss of life on both sides, Saddam Hussein remained a force to be reckoned with in the region and Saudi Arabia and Kuwait still function as mediaeval political systems with the trappings of modern prosperity. I suspect there may well still be a final act before the play is ended. I can only hope we get away as lightly the next time.

NOTES

1: Navy, Army, and Air Force Institute, which runs the supermarkets used by British army personnel and dependants in most garrison towns.
2: A battlegroup is an all arms grouping, ie comprising infantry, tanks, engineers, artillery etc, based on the headquarters of a battalion sized unit. The 4RTR battlegroup consisted of C and D Squadrons 4RTR, Letter A Company the 1st Battalion The Royal Greenjackets, a company of infantry from the 2nd Battalion The Parachute Regiment, and a number of other units and organisations making up a total of over 1000 men and over 200 vehicles.
3: Royal Electrical and Mechanical Engineers, the Corps responsible for, and expert in, all matters relating to the repair and maintenance of vehicles, weapons, and most other technical equipment and systems.
4: Nuclear, Biological, and Chemical. These instructors were trained in all aspects of personal and group protection against these particularly unpleasant weapons of war.
5: Interestingly enough, at some point in the proceedings the term BCR was deemed too emotive and replaced by the more euphemistic In Theatre Replacement (ITR), a move which caused much amusement to those concerned.
6: It is perhaps interesting to note that in 4RTR only three Senior

Non Commisioned Officers (SNCOs) volunteered for the Gulf compared to ten Officers. Most SNCOs were married at the time, while the bulk of the Officer volunteers were single, which may have something to do with it.

7: Now amalgamated with the Queen's Own Hussars to form the Queen's Royal Hussars.

8: Bovington Camp, Wareham, Dorset, is where the Royal Armoured Corps and the Royal Tank Regiment both have their Headquarters.

9: 20 November is Cambrai Day, commemorating the first day of the Battle of Cambrai in 1917 when the massed tanks of the Royal Tank Corps broke through the German front line near the town of the same name during the Great War.

10: Staff College, Camberley, where approximately 30% of army officers are trained for command and staff jobs in the ranks of Major and Lieutenant Colonel. Entrance is competitive, and it is very much "the right thing to do" for the ambitious career-minded officer. It is fatally flawed in that all assessment carried out to gauge a young officer's future potential is entirely subjective and his future progression is dependent on the approbation, or otherwise, of his instructors.

11: At this time operations which involved the deployment of British forces abroad were directed from either the Royal Navy HQ at Northwood (from where the Falklands war, Operation Corporate, had been directed), Army HQ at Wilton near Salisbury, or RAF HQ at High Wycombe. Generally speaking, whichever service was "leading" used its home HQ. As the RAF were first to be involved in the Gulf, their HQ at High Wycombe became the "de facto" joint HQ ("joint" meaning involving more than one service).

12: General Headquarters, where British Commanders-in-Chief were based during the Great War, was so remote from the front line that it frequently had little idea of what exactly was going on during operations. Although modern communications have improved things immeasurably, there were still occasions during the Gulf War when the same criticism could be made.

13: HQBFME was a Joint Headquarters, and as such had Navy, Army (or Land), and Air Cells as well as a Joint Operations Cell. I was to work in the Land Cell until operations were imminent, whereupon I moved to the Joint Ops Cell for the duration of the War.

14: Allowances was to become one of the major bones of contention during the Gulf War between those in the desert and those stationed in Riyadh, Bahrein, and elsewhere. Some of those who deployed to Riyadh in the very early days of the crisis were to save up to £7,500 from their allowances during their lengthy stay. It seemed mightily unfair to the fighting troops that those who were living in comparative luxury also benefitted financially. The fact that the RAF were first in was the main reason for our financial well being; they traditionally are much better at looking after themselves than the army. Had we been leading, I have no doubt that we would have lived in a tented camp throughout and eaten composite rations. Brigadier Christopher Hammerbeck, who commanded 4 Armoured Brigade, has been quoted as saying that there were only three occasions when he heard cheering in the desert; once when Riyadh suffered its first SCUD attack, once when the war ended, and most famously when it was learned that allowances were to stop in Riyadh!

15: SCUD was the generic name given to any medium to long range, surface to surface missile. The SCUD proper was such a missile of Soviet design which had been widely exported. The Iraqis had modified some to produce the Al Hussein and Al Abbas missiles, which had increased range but reduced warheads to compensate. It was these missiles which were used in the later attacks on Riyadh and elsewhere.
16: US security policy has divided the globe up into a number of Commands, each responsible for a particular area or function and commanded by a three or four star General. Kuwait, Saudi Arabia, and Iraq, amongst other countries, fell within the responsibility of CENTCOM, commanded by General Schwartzkopf.
17: General Officer Commanding.
18: So called because here the abysmal standard of Saudi driving could be seen at its very worst.
19: This was a mosque which sported two minaret towers which were remarkably like missiles about to be launched.
20: Now the Defence Research Agency.
21: Referred to on page 188 of his book.
22: Allowances were to start up again at the end of the war as numbers drew down, but I was long gone by then.
23: A Soviet made, hand-held anti tank rocket launcher, widely exported throughout the world and fairly effective in its day. Its presence in the Iraqi armoury was one of the reasons we were frantically uparmouring our Challengers and Warriors.
24: At this point we only had CNN in the Ops Room, and although it kept us in touch to a certain extent we longed for a more sophisticated coverage to keep us informed. Later on we got the BBC amongst great expressions of joy, and I don't think we ever looked at CNN again.

A Staff Officer's Account of the First Gulf War

25: A "sortie" is best defined as one aircraft taking off on a mission: 382 sorties means that 382 aircraft had taken to the air.
26: Ground attack version of the Panavia Tornado, jointly developed by Britain, Germany, and Italy. The RAF also operated the F3, an interceptor or air defence version. Large numbers of Tornados were also used by the Saudi Air Force with varying degrees of success.
27: Soviet built fighter, formidable enough in the hands of the right pilot but less threatening in the hands of the Iraqis.
28: US Navy and Marine Corps attack/fighter aircraft.
29: British/French single seat ground attack fighter.
30: Although we never really questioned where the information came from, we assumed that satellite surveillance detected missile launches in Iraq at this stage in the war.
31: As the name suggests, nerve agent attacks the central nervous system. When used as a weapon it is usually dispensed as a vapour and, when inhaled or ingested even in minute quantities, can kill very rapidly.
32: Nerve Agent Pre-treatment Set.
33: Combat Air Patrol.
34: There were usually two formal briefs given to the Commander each day, at 0800 and 1700.
35: US multi role, single engine fighter.
36: Version of the US Phantom fighter bomber equipped to attack and neutralise anti aircraft systems.
37: US Navy/Marine Corps attack aircraft.
38: US Marine Corps reconnaissance aircraft.
39: US built vintage attack aircraft, sometimes called the Skyhawk.
40: Put on our respirators.
41: After the war it was suggested that Patriot had only managed

to destroy about 30% of the SCUDs. Part of the problem would seem to have been caused by the propensity of the incoming missiles, modified by the Iraqis to extend their range, to break up towards the end of their trajectory. This provided the Patriot missile system with multiple targets and unfortunately it was not always the warhead of the SCUD which was destroyed.

42: Battle Damage Assessment.

43: Soviet built tank of 1960's vintage extensively exported round the world. Used by both Iraqi and Coalition forces during the Gulf War.

44: The elite of the Iraqi Army was the Republican Guard Force Command (RGFC) which was better trained and equipped than the rest of their ground forces. Reputedly fiercely loyal to Saddam Hussein, the Americans had identified the Divisions of the RGFC as Iraq's "operational centre of gravity" which if destroyed would lead inevitably to the defeat of all his ground units.

45: US Air Force's vintage strategic bomber, capable of carrying fifty-one 500 lb bombs per sortie against ground forces.

46: Electronic intelligence.

47: Surface to air missile.

48: ALARM stands for Air Launched Anti Radiation Missile, which homes in on the radiations of anti aircraft system radars.

49: Tactical Assembly Area.

50: The high losses sustained by the Tornado force in the early stages of the air war had eventually forced the RAF to abandon this mode of attack and adopt bombing from medium altitude, above the reach of most of the Iraqi anti aircraft armoury.

51: Observation Posts.

52: Ground attack aircraft known as the "Warthog" because of its unlovely appearance.
53: Special forces gunship version of the C 130 Hercules transport aircraft.
54: Killed in action and wounded in action.
55: Air launched anti ship missile built by British Aerospace.
56: The more usual British abbreviation for prisoners of war is PoW. However, the Americans used PW and we followed suit. It was further refined to include EPW, or enemy prisoners of war, to avoid confusion as to whether they were ours or theirs.
57: Joint Surveillance and Target Acquisition Radar System. This consists of a Boeing 707 kitted out with a variety of state of the art surveillance devices which allows the operators to have a more or less clear view of everything that moves on the ground over a large area. JSTARS was able to provide accurate information of events deep in Iraq without having to leave Saudi airspace.
58: Electronic warfare.
59: The US AH64 Apache attack helicopter, an extremely capable weapons system with an excellent night capability and extensive and comprehensive weapon load. Much envied by other nations, including the British who have now equipped the Army Air Corps with it.
60: This was extremely important for the air campaign for, despite the advances in all weather, day and night capabilities of modern aircraft, fine weather was still better for bombing and ground attack. The weather also had a significant effect on ground operations.
61: French Armoured Divisions are more akin in size to British Brigades – ie about 5000 men strong.

62: Greenwich Mean Time.
63: In other words, scientific investigation.
64: Subsequently claimed to be grossly exaggerated.
65: Not, in fact, true. US forces suffered a few tank casualties but the numbers were insignificant compared to the number of Iraqi tanks destroyed.
66: Rest and recreation.
67: The Americans had a similar but much better developed system which they call the After Action Review or AAR.
68: The Iraqis had set fire to many of the oil wells on retreating from Kuwait, and there was a permanent pall of black smoke over much of Kuwait which sometimes made flying quite tricky.
69: RAF transport helicopter, capable of carrying sixteen fully equipped troops or twenty on light scales.
70: Apparently one or two people tried to retain their hired vehicles beyond the end of the war, and rumour has it that more than one Range Rover was removed from containers on the docks just prior to shipping to the UK.
71: A popular method of so doing was by using plastic explosive concealed in the butts of AK47s.
72: FOOs are usually youngish officers or SNCOs in the Royal Artillery who are detached from the gun regiments and sent forward to support battlegroups in the contact battle. They have the training, specialised knowledge, and communications equipment to call for and direct artillery fire when asked to do so by local commanders.
73: Combined Cadet Force.
74: Hohne Ranges is the NATO tank firing range in northern Germany, habitually used by all British armoured units

stationed in Germany and shared with the Germans, Dutch, Belgians and so on. Castlemartin Ranges, in Pembrokeshire, is the equivalent in Britain.

75: In broad terms, officers usually join the army as Short Service or Regular Officers. Short Service Officers join for an initial three years, then may extend by mutual conset up to a maximum number of years or convert to a Regular Commission if deemed suitable. Regular Officers join as career men from the outset and can expect a career up to the age of fifty-five in normal circumstances.